SHRUBS &
SMALL TREES

SHRUBS &
SMALL TREES

GEOFFREY SMITH

*Flower drawings by Leslie Greenwood and
practical drawings by Ian Garrard*

GONDOLA

HAMLYN

First published in 1973 by The Hamlyn Publishing Group
for Collingridge Books
under the title Shrubs and Small Trees for Your Garden

Revised edition published 1981 by
The Hamlyn Publishing Group Limited
First published 1985 as a Hamlyn Gondola Book by
Hamlyn Publishing
a division of The Hamlyn Publishing Group Limited
Bridge House, London Road, Twickenham, Middlesex, England

ISBN 0 600 50083 7

Filmset in England by Photocomp Ltd

Printed in Italy

Contents

ACKNOWLEDGEMENTS

Cover photograph of the author by courtesy
of *Garden News*; other cover photographs
by Pat Brindley.
The publishers would like to thank the
following for supplying the colour photographs
used in this book: *Amateur Gardening*, Pat
Brindley, Robert Corbin, Bill Davidson, Valerie
Finnis, Iris Hardwick, Anthony Huxley, Elsa
Megson, Robert Pearson, The Harry Smith
Horticultural Photographic Collection.

Colour Illustrations

Penzance Briar rose

CONVERSION CHARTS

Length				Weight	
$\frac{1}{2}$ in	1 cm	2 ft	0·6 m	$\frac{1}{2}$ oz	14 g
1 in	2·5 cm	3 ft	0·9 m	1 oz	28 g
2 in	5 cm	4 ft	1·2 m	2 oz	56 g
3 in	8 cm	5 ft	1·5 m	3 oz	85 g
4 in	10 cm	6 ft	1·8 m	4 oz	113 g
5 in	13 cm	7 ft	2·1 m	5 oz	142 g
6 in	15 cm	8 ft	2·5 m	6 oz	170 g
7 in	18 cm	9 ft	2·7 m	7 oz	198 g
8 in	20 cm	10 ft	3·0 m	8 oz	226 g
9 in	23 cm	15 ft	4·5 m	16 oz (1 lb)	454 g
10 in	25 cm	20 ft	6·0 m	2·2 lb	1 kg
11 in	28 cm	50 ft	15·2 m		
12 in (1 ft)	30 cm	100 ft	30·5 m		

Introduction

No special qualifications are needed to become a gardener, just an interest in plants. Certainly there are opportunities enough for the whole gamut of gardeners to indulge their particular interests, from the dedicatedly intense to the dilettante potterer. Some of the most enthusiastic gardeners find in the cultivation of soil an outlet for the peasant instinct buried deep inside every human being and a satisfying collection of plants can be built up within the compass of the smallest garden. If it were possible to lay down a set of rules to be followed to achieve a given goal, be it a four-pound onion, or a perfectly symmetrical silver fir, most of the pleasure of anticipation would be removed. Indeed, I look back over the thirty-three years which I have spent as a professional gardener, and find in them a compendium of trial and error. There are so many factors beyond our control that the element of chance will never be completely eliminated.

This book is a chronicle of personal experiences, success and failure. Without the failures, success when finally achieved would have lost much of its savour. Gardening consists of long periods of routine toil interspersed with moments of such sublime beauty that all the digging, weeding, and downright anxiety are forgotten. No-one knows just when one of these never-to-be forgotten experiences will occur. A sudden break in the clouds to allow a shaft of sunlight to bring out a hitherto unremarked beauty in leaf or flower is not something we can organise, then invite friends to witness. Such moments are personal, bought by experience, often at the cost of considerable effort, but they enrich life to an extent which only those who grow plants can appreciate.

No-one can evaluate the fascination of gardening until they begin to explore the world of plants. By taking advantage of the recorded experience of others the beginner will avoid the worst pitfalls.

Shrubs and trees are the ultimate of gardening endeavour, a permanent record of the years spent in their cultivation. Trees I planted thirty-five years ago on a wind-swept heather-grown moorland will not reach maturity until after my horticultural efforts are long forgotten. I have had the pleasure of seeing them through the important formative years, and take a delight in anticipating the joy their beauty will bring to future generations of plant lovers.

Possibly this book will encourage someone somewhere to plant a tree or a shrub, so that they too will experience the joys and anxieties of watching it through the seasons. There is *nothing* quite so rewarding.

Geoffrey Smith

Part 1

Creating Garden Features

Hedging Plants

Ground Cover Plants

Tree Silhouettes

Conifers

Climbers and Wall Plants

Creating Garden Features

As the rash of tarmacadam and concrete spreads to hide the soft green contours of rural Britain, so will an increasingly office-bound community turn to their gardens for a place in which to relax. Gardening is a healthy, creative hobby with many rewards and a well-planned and tended garden can provide its owner with a peaceful setting in which he can spend many happy hours.

The demands on the limited amount of land available for housing developments continue to increase and inevitably gardens will become smaller, at least those the majority of amateur gardeners can afford. To achieve a balanced design which, with the passage of time, will blend into a composite whole requires a sympathetic understanding of both soil and plants. Once this knowledge has been attained it will give immense satisfaction.

Without doubt, for anyone with limited time, shrubs are the most practical method of achieving a creditable garden with minimum effort. This does not mean that once planted up nothing more is required from the person responsible except the purchase of a deckchair and sunshade. A conifer with all the lower branches killed by weeds allowed to grow unchecked around it is not to be compared with a specimen furnished to soil level with healthy foliage. Initially the garden will have a very lean unfinished look, but only for one or two seasons and these formative years are of vital importance if the shrubs are to attain in maturity their full potential.

An argument frequently put forward against a garden devoted entirely to shrubs is that each individual has only one season of show. This supposition betrays the most appalling ignorance. The Honeysuckle Azalea, *Rhododendron luteum,* becomes a mound of funnel-shaped, sweetly scented flowers in spring while in autumn this most lovely shrub makes a colour carnival as the foliage changes to orange-crimson, even deep wine purple. Or possibly a better example would be *Amelanchier lamarckii* which has leaves of copper red in spring, then white flowers, and finally during October a rich colouration of dying leaves. A well-designed shrub border should be a garden for all seasons with the contrasting of deciduous and evergreen genera, balanced so that even in the austere aridity of December the picture created is sufficiently inviting to encourage a closer inspection.

I know from experience just how difficult gardening on a very exposed site can be. For twenty years I worked to transform a hillside above Harrogate, Yorkshire with an uninterrupted view of the Pennines to the west. At times when the thick glacial clay was at its most affectionately clinging, or when in July I watched dahlias, roses, and delphiniums being torn to shreds by a capricious wind, the thought of letting heather and bracken take over once more crossed my mind. However, the intervening years have seen hedges grow to provide shelter and a stand of young spruce now blocks the westerly wind tunnel. The clay has improved to the extent that, though still powerfully adhesive, the plants thrive on the strong diet.

Rhododendron luteum

Planning and Preparation

I have never, in spite of over thirty-five years of concentrated effort, achieved my perfect garden and I hope I never will. Every empty plot becomes a challenge, a tapestry to be woven in plant patterns which, because of the wealth of different material available, are capable of a million permutations.

I formed a habit many years ago, when first starting to visit gardens, of superimposing my own design over that already in existence, even to the extent of sketching it on a drawing pad. Gradually I discovered that the gardens which pleased me best were not those which were merely an enormous collection of plants, or vast estates, but rather those in which the architect or landscape designer had achieved simplicity so that the eye was soothed not over stimulated.

One should always try to work with the land, utilising to the fullest extent any natural features. A stream is a great asset to the garden designer for water brings movement and extends the range of plantings. A gentle slope can become a rock or heather garden, while a steeper incline can be broken up with terraces; stone is beautiful if used discreetly in broad steps and gentle curving walls. There may be a superb view which can be drawn into the garden by a framework of muted plantings which lead the eye to the landscape beyond the boundary.

There is the same initial excitement of anticipation when moving into a house with the garden already established. Spend the first twelve months trying to find out precisely what the plot contains for there may be valuable shrubs hidden behind the anonymity of leafless branches. Unfortunately, most garden owners conclude the previous occupiers to be horticultural morons and set about erasing every sign of their presence with a vigorous enthusiasm. Assume instead that the original design was in the nature of a masterpiece, then embellish or delete so that the main features become an expression of your own artistic sense.

Only when it is obvious that the garden is incapable of supporting them or they are obviously moribund should any trees be removed. Anyone with a small garden dominated by a sycamore, chestnut, ash or beech will understand how difficult gardening can be with both root competition and shade of the calibre which these trees provide. However, I do emphasise that only after careful consideration should any major onslaught be made for seventy years of growth can be destroyed in an hour.

The crime I once committed through youthful ignorance cured me for all time of an impetuous approach to garden landscape. Once I had decided on gardening as a career, my father suggested that I should be responsible for the garden, over an acre in extent, which lay in the shelter of a fold in the Yorkshire Dales just below the moors. I was very much a novice, depending on annuals for a quick return for my labours. A beautiful clipped yew planted when the house was built and a golden chamaecyparis were central features of the house frontage. Anything which took up space capable of supporting a marigold or godetia was anathema to me so one day when father was away I uprooted both these patriarchs on to the bonfire. No one in that quiet Dales village spoke to me for a week. They were all too busy sympathising with my parents for having produced such a wayward son. The many hundred trees I have planted since have not erased the feeling of guilt this piece of vandalism burdened me with.

There are many pitfalls to trap the unwary but these can be avoided by exercising a little care. The whole future of the garden should be one of expanding interest which can only be achieved by careful planning right from the beginning. A broad overall plan is essential so try to rough out on paper the ideas which in due course will become a practical reality. Spend several evenings sketching in different designs, planning the plantings, even drawing in the shapes of the plants needed to give the best contrast of shape or foliage. Study the garden from the main windows of the house, then take a back siting from the garden, until gradually the two become one single unit; the garden another room to be decorated, then furnished. By detailed study every aspect of soil, exposure, even sunlight and shade become fixed in the mind so that each becomes an asset not a liability.

A plant only achieves its full potential when planted under the conditions which suit it best and this all-important factor must be taken into consideration when choosing and buying plants for the garden. A comprehensive list of the shrubs and small trees which have adapted themselves to suit every set of conditions which are likely to be encountered by the garden maker can be found at the back of this book. (Pages 163–167).

Some check must be made to ascertain if the soil is acid or alkaline as the results of this simple test will have a profound influence on the type of plants chosen. The local Horticultural Officer will have a complete test done or a soil-testing kit can be bought fairly cheaply from any sundriesman. It is quite simple and often very interesting to use one of these kits. The acid/

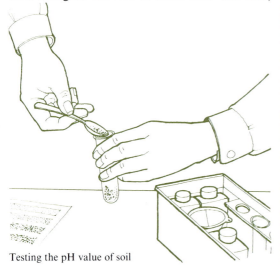

Testing the pH value of soil

alkaline reaction of the soil is expressed as the pH value – pH7 is neutral being neither acid nor alkaline while figures below 7 show increasing degrees of acidity and above 7 increasing degrees of alkalinity. Most plants will grow in soils within a range between pH6 and 7.

An exact reading is not necessary, however, just a guide as to whether the soil contains lime or not. Our gardening would be so much easier if we contented ourselves with growing only those plants which were adapted to our own particular soil and climate.

Whatever the conditions, however, no shrub will succeed unless planted in a well-prepared soil. There is no short cut to soil fertility, no chemical magic to change overnight a sterile desert into a Garden of Eden, no matter how hard the manufacturers advertise their individual wares.

Drainage must be a primary concern except when the garden is sited on a sandy soil when the problem will be water retention rather than draining an excess away. Some gardens have a system of tile drainage which will cope adequately with any excess rain, short of a tropical thunderstorm.

The first rains of winter will soon discover any defects in the drainage. If water stands in puddles round the rose beds or on the lawns it may be that the existing drains are blocked or damaged. An afternoon's work with a set of jointed rods will clear most obstructions. In extreme cases a completely new system of land tiles must be laid. On clay these should be put down 30 to 36 in., covered with a layer of gravel, then by the excavated soil.

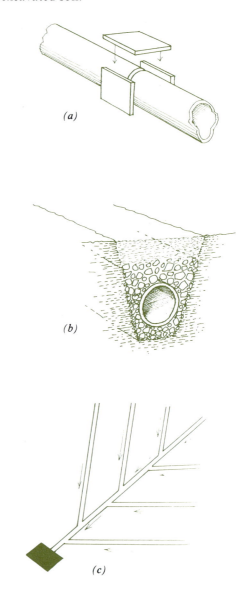

(a) A junction protected with slates prevents the entry of silt
(b) A section through a drain
(c) The herring-bone system of drainage ensures the removal of excess water

There are less laborious methods of removing surplus moisture. Pipes made of plastic can be drawn into the required depth by a heavy tractor. If the sub-soil is free from stones a system of mole drains will function adequately for twenty years or more. These are made by a tractor pulling a special plough which leaves a water channel through the clay approximately 24 in. down. Having struggled in one corner of my own garden with a badly drained soil I am now convinced that unless surplus moisture is removed the full pleasure of gardening can never be enjoyed.

Nothing will make a newcomer to gardening an outcast of society quicker than to be continually borrowing tools. There is no need, however, to rush into buying one of everything and a good collection can be built up slowly as required; some being needed immediately while others can wait for a birthday. A good spade must head the list and a garden fork will also be needed practically from the beginning to deal with perennial weeds and in helping to break down the soil before planting. A round-pronged, general-purpose fork gives me the best service.

Transporting of heavy materials is impossible without a wheelbarrow. Buy a strongly built large capacity model, the type used on building sites with an inflatable wheel is excellent value but might be beyond the strength of a woman. The lighter aluminium version is a good substitute, but choose one with a broad wheel as the narrow-wheeled versions are impossible to push on soft ground and will leave unsightly ridges across the smooth lawn.

I do not like using either a spade or a fork around newly planted shrubs, and even less near mature specimens. A three-pronged, long-handled cultivator is my favourite tool during the summer as it cleans and aerates the soil without disturbing the shrubs' roots.

During prolonged wet weather a heavy crop of weeds may develop and an excursion with a broad-bladed hoe on the first bright sunny day is the best way to clear this particular nuisance. I choose the blade, then bend it in a vice until, when fitted with a handle, it sits flat in a working position while my back remains comfortably straight. I gave up bending to push hoes many years ago.

A rake is a refinement and not really essential. A fork or cultivator will do the necessary levelling off of the soil before planting. A reel and line will be needed to ensure that the various hedges are laid straight and true. Few people have a reliable enough eye to work without one.

I always buy the best tools which available

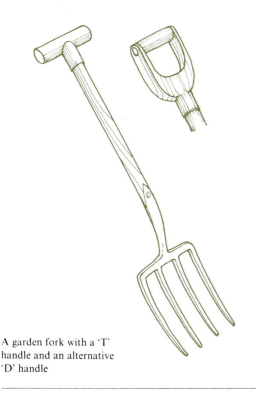

A garden fork with a 'T' handle and an alternative 'D' handle

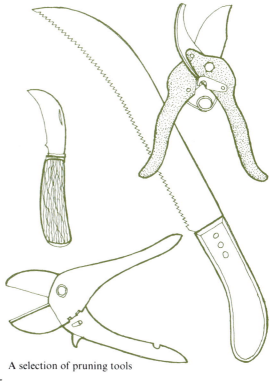

A selection of pruning tools

funds permit, especially when it comes to secateurs and pruning saw, but the best is not always the most expensive. Find out which secateurs the nearest professional is using, then buy those. A good knife is something no gardener is ever without. I have one purchased many years ago which will give me a lifetime service. The tools described will make up a modest collection and they will certainly be adequate to maintain the largest shrub border. To the basic outfit could be added a manure fork and shovel which would make the annual mulching of the border with manure or compost rather less of a labour.

At long last the gardener can don heavy boots and take a spade in hand to make a start on preparing the soil to receive the chosen shrubs. Newly planted shrubs will establish rapidly if they are provided with a soil which has been worked some fifteen inches deep. First take out a trench across one end 15 in. wide, placing the soil to one side for filling up the final trench when the work is completed. Into the bottom fork a generous dressing of whatever organic matter is available. Those living in a town will find a mixture of coarse bonemeal and peat the cleanest to handle. A further dressing mixed with the top spadeful leaves a beautifully worked soil into which the roots can penetrate freely.

Organic matter may be obtained in the form of compost, farm manure, spent hops, the unsaleable refuse from a greengrocers, peat, in fact anything which is non-toxic to plants and which will rot down. I garden on hungry wet clay, but after 17 years of mulching this has the rich spongy texture of home-made Christmas pudding. Organic matter is broken down by the flora and fauna in the soil to leave a black residue known as humus which is immensely important to the health of the soil. Humus improves the water holding capacity and, at the same time, the drainage. By providing food for bacteria this black spongy substance assists in releasing suitable plant foods which otherwise would be unavailable, and stops them from being removed too rapidly by leaching. Annual dressings of organic matter, once the shrubs are planted, maintain the humus essential to a healthy soil. One of the contradictions of gardening is that organic matter is the finest conditioner for both light and heavy soils. With the former it increases the water holding and nutrient capacity; with the latter it facilitates the aeration and drainage by opening up the tightly packed particles. Try to get all the rough digging done in the autumn so that the frost can break down the heavy clods to give a fine workable tilth by the time spring arrives.

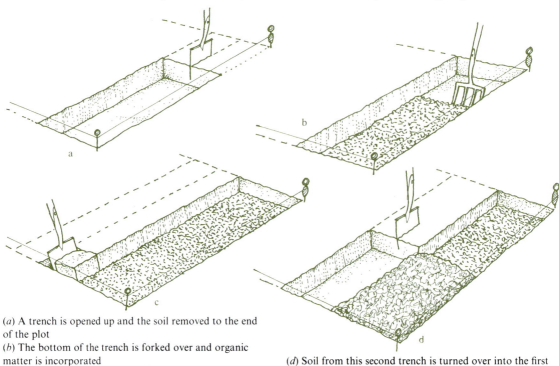

(*a*) A trench is opened up and the soil removed to the end of the plot
(*b*) The bottom of the trench is forked over and organic matter is incorporated
(*c*) A further trench of the same dimensions is marked out
(*d*) Soil from this second trench is turned over into the first trench and so on until the whole plot has been dug over

Where the planting is being done into individual holes without digging the whole area, the same procedure is adopted only the organic matter used must be well rotted. Remove the existing soil to a depth of 15 to 18 in., mix in the compost and if the soil is heavy a dressing of coarse sand. Where the border is rough dug as previously described then left to weather the sand is unnecessary.

I look back with pleasure on long winter evenings spent completely oblivious to the passing of time, planning shrub border after shrub border. After careful observations, many visits to new gardens, and discussions with beginners to gardening, I am convinced that one of the commonest mistakes and the most expensive is to overplant. This is not quite so serious if done deliberately to achieve a mature well-furnished effect quickly by using three plants of the same species but it requires the confidence that one's strength of mind will be equal to the task of removing two before the struggle for existence ruins all three.

An example of this type of planting might be to put in three *Cytisus albus* because one alone would look a very wan orphan for two or three years. Cytisus is easy to propagate so before removing the unwanted bushes they could provide cuttings for extending still further the shrub planting elsewhere in the garden. I would never use expensive shrubs for this filler technique unless, like rhododendrons, they transplanted easily and could be utilised elsewhere in the garden.

Choosing a day when the soil is dry or hard frozen enough not to be damaged, the planting ideas which have been worked out in detail on paper can be pegged out on the site. To avoid referring repeatedly to a plan I print the name of each shrub in large capitals on a postcard and then pin this on a plant stake or cane. At this stage it is invaluable if some member of the family can be called in to assist as general factotum to move the stakes about as directed.

An idea of the ultimate spread of the bush or tree is desirable as, unfortunately, height alone is no guide; some being upright in growth while others sprawl elegantly over square yards of garden. An example of this very factor can be found in two excellent berberis. *Berberis* x *stenophylla* is a spreading ground hog which needs 8 to 10 ft. of elbow room whereas an attractive specimen of *B.* x *lologensis* in my own

garden has grown to only 5 ft. in 16 years and spread out to occupy a modest square yard of soil. Fortunately the *B.* x *stenophylla* can be restrained by pruning without destroying its characteristic shape, but this does not apply by any means to all invasive shrubs. I would rather be overgenerous in the matter of space than niggardly for gaps can be filled with bulbs or choice herbaceous perennials.

Planting

Planting is almost a ritual with me; shrubs are expensive so every care is taken to ensure success. Into the wheelbarrow go spade, fork, string, a sharp knife or secateurs, and a tin of sealing compound for treating large cuts or damaged bark. I return immediately for a barrowload of riddled soil mixed with bonemeal for working around the fine roots.

Unless absolutely essential I avoid staking as this makes the plant lazy about forming roots. I made this discovery when I was given two standards of *Crataegus oxyacantha* Double Crimson Thorn 12 years ago. One I planted in my own shrub border while the other went into what used to be the hen field and is now a small wood. The garden specimen was staked and still needs support but the other took pot luck and stands firm to the four winds.

In winter my gardening continues with unabated vigour, but conversationally rather than physically. Each week there are meetings to attend, and always the talk is of gardens and plants. One evening the importance of container-

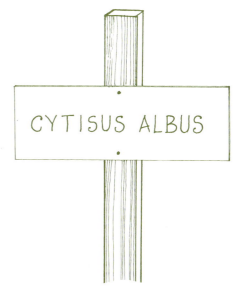

grown shrubs was reviewed in some detail with the professionals, a minority group on this occasion, firm in their conviction that these have proved of benefit to both nurseryman and amateur gardener. Now the planting season need not be restricted to the period between October and early May. The roots are not exposed to all the dehydration inevitable when the shrubs are despatched by road or rail, some-times taking weeks to reach their destination. With container-grown plants even a magnolia may be transferred to the garden in full bloom. There is no check to the most delicate genera, for with moderate care the root system is undisturbed and the shrub is unaware of the move. Above all exact colour of foliage or flower can be studied before buying so that attractive blends and contrasts may be achieved with the attendant pleasure of seeing the pattern grow as the work proceeds. Container-grown shrubs can cost rather more than those produced by orthodox open-ground methods, but the extra expense is in most cases justified by the results. Make certain when buying that the shrubs are container grown and not just potted up for the occasion or the soil just falls away from the roots at planting time.

My own views on the correct season for planting open-ground-raised shrubs fluctuate with the weather. In a wet season I have success-fully moved rhododendrons, junipers, and laurel in June and July. However, pinned down to a single season I would settle for early spring. Winters on my exposed garden can be brutal in the extreme and linked with a cold wet clay soil the shock is too much for all but the most robust genera. I prefer to let the nurseryman carry my charges through the worst months, then as the soil warms give me the responsibility. There are hazards, late frosts, drought, searing winds, but these can be mitigated by rough shelters of polythene.

The ideal planting day is easily defined, but rarely do soil and weather see fit to combine and assist the gardener in this respect. Only in exceptional circumstances should work proceed when the soil is so wet that large clods adhere to the boots. Choose a day when the stubbornest clay runs like silk from the spade, then fine root hairs can be firmed into position with the least damage. I prefer a dull humid day if there are several shrubs to plant up as strong winds or bright sunshine will dry exposed roots in a matter of minutes. Rarely is the dull humid day followed by a frost at night, rather as the day-light fades comes a warm soaking rain to complete the soil firming in the best manner.

Parcels of shrubs always seem to arrive at the most inconvenient times, even when I specify early spring delivery. Sometimes the garden is deep under snow, at others hard or water-logged, making immediate planting impossible. When frost or snow are the limiting factors, open the top of the parcel but leave the roots intact as packed by the nursery, and stand the package in a frost-free shed until the weather moderates. When excessive wet or pressure of work prevent the shrubs going directly into their

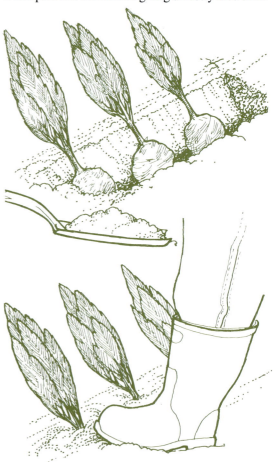

Heeling in shrubs which arrive before they can be planted into their permanent positions. A trench is taken out and the shrubs are lined out. The soil is then replaced and lightly firmed

permanent positions then they must be heeled in on a sheltered border. Take out a trench large enough to accommodate the roots without damage. One side of the trench may be vertical; the other, against which the plants will lean, is angled at 45 degrees. The stems rest on the sloping side which completely obviates any question of windrock. The soil is then replaced over the roots and lightly firmed, not hammered down solid.

When suitable weather for planting at last arrives, collect the shrubs from the heeling-in ground, making certain the roots do not dry out by wrapping them in a wet piece of sacking. I did a little experiment with some seedling rowan to find out just how much difference keeping the roots moist or letting them dry out made to a shrub's chances of survival. In fact, I proved to my own satisfaction that just five minutes exposure to a drying March wind reduces the viability of woody plants appreciably. In the case of conifers the dehydration proved fatal in one out of every four seedling thuja lined out as a hedge.

If the border has been well prepared, digging the planting hole will be a simple business. It should be large enough to take the roots of the tree or shrub well spread out. If a stake is necessary put in a cane to mark the place where it can be driven home without damaging the roots. This must, of course, be on the windward side, usually the west, so there is less chance of the stem being chafed by blowing on to the stake. People who advise putting the stake in position before planting may be correct, but if the stake interferes with firming I leave it until this most important task is done. When the hole is ready, trim any damaged roots back to sound wood. Secateurs are the best tool for doing this unless you have a very sharp knife. With roses, malus and indeed most shrubs, unless the roots are fleshy as in magnolia, I tip back even the undamaged roots to encourage the formation of the fibrous feeding roots essential for quick establishment.

No top pruning should be necessary if the nurseryman has done his work well. Some twigs or even branches may have been damaged in transit; cut these back into sound wood then treat the wounds with a sealing compound of Stockholm tar or Arbrex. When training in the nursery has been neglected there may be crossing or badly placed branches to cut away but if this happens often I would try another nursery with more interest in the plants they offer for sale.

Carefully place the shrub into the planting hole and with fingers work in the riddled soil, firming gently so that each root is in full and intimate

Planting a shrub. The stick indicates to the planter the correct planting depth

contact with the soil and there are no air pockets left to gather stagnant air and moisture. Finally fill in with excavated soil up to the mark on the stem which indicates the depth of the original planting in the nursery. Rhododendrons are the exception to the rule as they should be high planted and then well mulched with compost or peat. This applies on all but the lightest soils as rhododendrons are surface rooting. Planted deep the roots may die through lack of air although frequently the more determined species survive by growing a new root system at soil level. Heathers should be inserted a little deeper so that the bottoms of the branches are well covered. These will root in due course to give greatly increased vigour.

I do not leap about on the soil in imitation of a Dervish dancer until it is packed like adobe mud. Moderation in all things; a gentle firming of the lower levels is enough and the top layer should be left loose so that the rain can penetrate easily. Unless the soil is dry, watering in can usually be left to our obliging climate. Evergreens, especially conifers, are the exception. I water these overhead on every dry day, thoroughly wetting the foliage. A generous moisture-conserving mulch completes the job and the spade can then be cleaned and returned to the shed. I included the fork because with some shrubs the roots are so deep and strong that it is sometimes necessary to break up the bottom

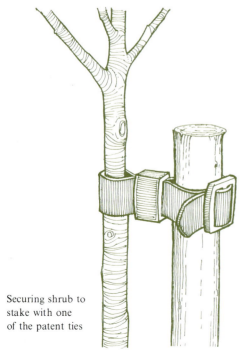

Securing shrub to
stake with one
of the patent ties

of the hole with the fork, working in some compost at the same time.

The cane can then be removed and a neat but solid stake driven home. I hate to see makeshift staking as it ruins the look of the whole garden. Stake and tree can be joined with any one of the dozen or so patent ties on the market which considerably reduces the risk of either damaging the stem, or worse still strangling the plant altogether.

Aftercare

Each year, unless the soil is very good, a feed of complete fertiliser followed by a thick mulch improves the fertility and suppresses weeds. If the mulch is composed of manure or other easily rotted material nothing more needs to be done, but with straw, cotton seed waste, or shoddy, add extra nitrogen to the feed or the shrubs will show a deficiency. When mulching with a good compost is carried out regularly each year the annual feed can be dropped after two applications. The mulch should be applied when the soil is thoroughly moist. The material used should be of a loose open nature so as not to cut off the air to the shrubs' roots.

Blackbirds can be a problem as they look on the mulch as their personal larder to be investigated at regular intervals with the result that it is frequently scattered all over the path or lawn. A layer of sand curbs their enthusiasm and holds the mulch down.

A great deal of money is spent each year on fertilisers, some of which I am sure would be better invested in buying compost bins. I use a balanced feed as a complement to the organic mulch, not as a substitute for it. Possibly the safest general feeds are those based on organic substances which in addition to feeding have no detrimental effect on soil texture. The release of the nitrogen, phosphates and potash takes place over a long period so that very little is lost by the plant through being leached away in soil drainage.

Bonemeal, hoof and horn, and fish meal, together with mixtures based on seaweed can be used over almost the whole garden without fear of harmful side effects. Usually, as well as the nitrogen, phosphates and potash, they contain a whole series of trace elements which though required by the plants in parts per million rather than ounces per square yard are never the less

Mulching

essential if the plants are to grow well.

All compound fertilisers have a statutory analysis printed on the container. By the condition of the plants, a gardener decides what they need to achieve a balanced growth and buys accordingly. Nitrogen encourages soft vigorous growth and deepens the colour of the foliage. An excess is harmful, increasing susceptibility to disease or damage by frost. Nitrogenous fertilisers are usually quickly leached out of the soil so they should be applied in small quantities at regular intervals where necessary.

The bones of animals when steamed and finely ground are a valuable source of phosphates. The breakdown is slow so that the food is released over a long period. Plants short of phosphates usually have a poorly developed root system and basic slag or superphosphate of lime can be used to correct an obvious deficiency quickly.

Potash encourages fruit production, intensifies flower colours and hardens growth. This is an over simplification, but basically true. Wood ash contains a small percentage of potassium, but the form in which the element is usually applied to the soil is as sulphate or muriate of potash. An excess of nitrogen can be balanced by applying extra potash. Autumn-colouring shrubs like photinia and acers should get extra potash as this will give the scarlets, yellows and purples added lustre.

Either forking or digging between established shrubs is not a practice to be recommended, for no matter how carefully employed there must be some root damage. The mulch keeps the soil well aerated while the weeds can be discouraged by the hand cultivator or a push hoe. Neither of these tools will penetrate to a sufficient depth to touch the roots.

There are, of course, the paraquat-based chemical weedkillers which can be used amongst established shrubs if the border is very dirty. Providing these do not come into contact with the leaves they will not harm the cultivated plants. The chemical acts only through the chlorophyll in the leaves so it can be sprayed right up the stems of the shrubs.

Only in extreme cases do I resort to spraying as a control for pests or diseases. Even then only the chemicals which are absolutely harmless to other wild life are used. On land newly broken in from pasture, wireworms, cockchafer grubs, or cutworms may prove troublesome. Trapping, handpicking, regular hoeing and in my garden a resident hedgehog are sufficient to keep all three pests well within bounds. There are special dusts on the market, but I avoid using them if at all possible.

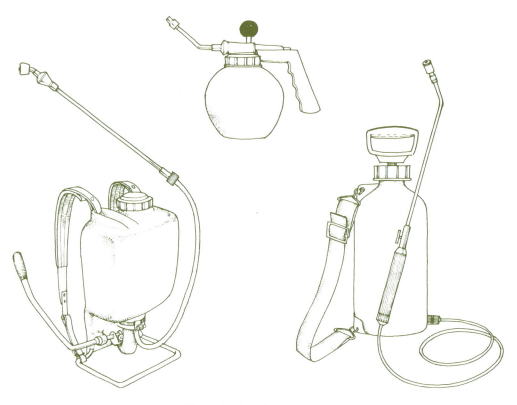

Three different kinds of chemical sprayers

Few shrubs can amass such an array of blackfly as the viburnums and these must be dealt with, for over two or three years the shrub will be reduced to a mass of stunted twisted twig-like growths. Spraying commences as the leaves unfurl with a derris-pyrethrum pesticide, plus a liquid soap which acts as a spreader and increases the efficiency of the chemical, and continues until late June. Shrub roses, flowering currants and some other inhabitants of the garden are prone to give board to greenfly. The spray advised for the blackfly will control them also. Indeed, it seems that there is a spray for everything likely to infest the garden from aphids to stray cats and dogs. Choose those which will only kill the pest or in the case of domestic animals repel them. Red spider mite may cause damage on dwarf conifers but can be controlled with malathion or similar chemical. Tortrix, sawfly and other caterpillars are rarely a problem. Derris and soft soap is a sufficiently potent repellent.

Fungus diseases may be a nuisance on wet or similarly inhospitable soils but rarely make inroads in a well-tended garden. Honey fungus which finds harbourage in old tree stumps or rotting posts can be expelled by removing any decaying tree or shrub remains to the bonfire. Coral spot, which shows on infected twigs as bright pink or orange pustules, usually indicates a shrub already weakened from some other cause. All dead or infected wood should be cut and burned. Treat wounds with Stockholm tar or Arbrex. Make sure fence posts, pergolas and other wooden structures are treated with a

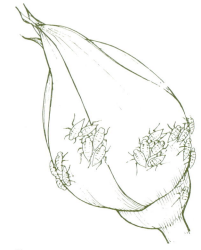

Greenflies on a rose

preservative or they can be a source of infection.

Botrytis, a fungus which in certain years may prove troublesome, usually starts in dead leaves. If these are removed and the shrub is treated with one of the sulphur-based sprays the infection will not spread. Mildew, black spot and rust are a particular problem where roses are grown in any quantity. I use sulphur for the mildew, and one of the dozen or so sprays on offer made specifically to control the other two.

I hesitate to introduce the thought that on occasions birds or animals can be a nuisance, and even then usually manufacture an excuse for their behaviour. Rabbits can be fenced out, although with enough dogs and cats about the garden only the most foolhardy rodent dare show its teeth. Moles will seek less aromatic pastures if moth balls or creosote are inserted into the runs at intervals. Voles and woodmice can be evicted in a similar fashion but a resident kestrel employed full time is more effective I have discovered! Bullfinches are the worst pest in this garden, their depredations have killed several full grown cherries and we rarely get any flowers on the others. Short of shooting, the gardener must resort to foul-tasting sprays, or netting the trees.

Renovating existing borders

Occasionally a border is neglected due to lack of interest or ability to cope on the part of the previous owner, and drastic renovations are necessary. Go over the border naming as many of the inhabitants as you can and when in doubt get an expert to advise you.

Experience has taught me that it is better to remove the short-lived shrubs like cytisus, cistus and roses completely. After a few years of neglect these are just clutter and will hamper the work of rehabilitation. Important slow-growing shrubs like magnolia, parrotia and hamamelis must be marked so that they are not expelled by accident. Others which transplant readily such as rhododendrons and chamaecyparis can be removed to leave only the bare framework. It is surprising how much easier reclamation proves to be when tackled in a systematic manner. Even more surprising are the things discovered in the overgrown border, from old bicycle frames to the summer house hidden under a mass of *Clematis montana* and ivy.

Pruning can be phased out over two years so that the effects are not drastically obvious or the shock unbearable to the plants. By careful feeding, manuring and pruning, an apparently derelict border can be restored.

Pruning

Many gardeners are inclined to worry too much about this aspect of tree and shrub cultivation for providing a few simple rules are followed pruning is a comparatively easy task. Many shrubs need little or no pruning beyond a clean up of dead, damaged or overcrowded wood. The aim should be to preserve the characteristic outline of the plant and this means doing only sufficient cutting to maintain it in good health, combined with maximum production of colour be it flower, berry, leaf or stem. Pruning is most important in the early years of a plant's life when a little discreet cutting is required to create a good overall shape.

A sharp saw, well-maintained pair of secateurs, and a razor-edged knife are prime essentials. I also include as supplementary equipment a tin of Stockholm tar and a brush for treating cut surfaces if any very large branches have to be cut away.

Try wherever possible to cut each branch away cleanly, leaving no stumps as these may harbour pests and diseases. This is particularly important with evergreens, magnolias and cherries. Where the complete removal of a branch is not practicable or desirable, always cut to an outward-facing bud, the wound sloping up to leave the bud at the apex. Removal of heavier branches must be done with a saw making the cut as close to the main stem as possible. I always round the rough edges afterwards with a knife before treating the exposed surface with a suitable protective covering. Above all make the cuts clean, not ragged, as they heal so much quicker leaving little or no scar.

Anyone faced with the task of maintaining a well-stocked shrub border should familiarise themselves first with the time of flowering. A forsythia needs altogether different treatment to that which is given to a hydrangea. Careless uninformed pruning can ruin an expensive shrub beyond all hope of recovery. Some idea of what a perfect specimen of the shrub to be treated should look like in maturity is also necessary, then pruning can be aimed at preserving and emphasising the characteristic outline.

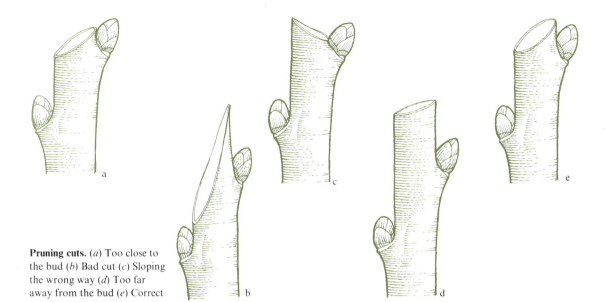

Pruning cuts. (*a*) Too close to the bud (*b*) Bad cut (*c*) Sloping the wrong way (*d*) Too far away from the bud (*e*) Correct

Evergreen shrubs, as for example rhododendron, berberis, and garrya, do not need regular or systematic pruning. Occasionally they are forced out of shape by wind or broken by snow, become thin or grown out, then the gardener must use secateurs and saw to restore equilibrium. I always carry out heavy pruning of evergreens just before growth commences in the spring. This stimulates growth just when conditions are the most favourable. Light pruning, frequently required to keep *Berberis* x *stenophylla* or escallonia within their prescribed limits, should be performed immediately after flowering. Heathers, both erica and calluna, should be trimmed with a pair of garden shears immediately the flowers fade. This prevents the plants becoming straggly and untidy. Sheep perform the same functional pruning in the wild, keeping the heather in hard compact mounds and the picture of health. Do not try to reclaim worn out plants by hard pruning. Heathers should not be clipped back lower than the wood of the previous season.

Deciduous shrubs offer a little more scope to the surgically minded. Pruning is carried out in accordance with the flowering season of the plant concerned which requires a certain basic interest in the individual inhabitants of the shrub border. Though the division is arbitrary, shrubs can be split into two groups; those which flower in the summer on the current season's growth, and the second group which is much larger and includes all the early-flowering shrubs

which contribute so much to the beauty of springtime. They flower on wood made the previous year, producing flower buds before the onset of winter which remain dormant until spring, whereas with the first group, growth and flowering take place the same year. Flowering is, in fact, the climax of the season's growth.

When pruning either group becomes necessary it should be so arranged as to encourage and not reduce flowering. Complete the work so that the shrub has the maximum period of growth before the next flowering season comes round. Group one, whose flowers are carried as a climax to the current season's growth, may be pruned at any time during the winter until just before growth begins in the spring. *Buddleia davidii* and its numerous varieties, *Spiraea japonica,* caryopteris, hypericum and *Hydrangea paniculata* flower profusely if cut hard back to within three or four buds of the old wood. If the severity of the pruning is varied in the case of *Hypericum patulum* then the time of flowering is staggered. Pruned lightly the flowers come in July on 4-ft. stems, a little harder the first flush opens in August, cut to soil level it makes a dome-shaped mound 18 to 24 in. massed high with flowers.

The second group of shrubs which flower in spring and early summer on wood formed the previous season such as forsythia, ribes, and philadelphus are pruned immediately after flowering has finished. Remove old worn out wood to encourage the growth of strong healthy

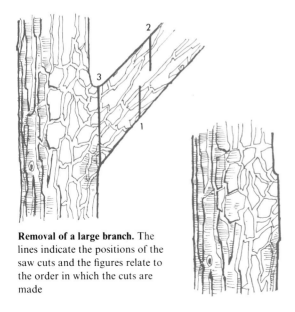

Removal of a large branch. The lines indicate the positions of the saw cuts and the figures relate to the order in which the cuts are made

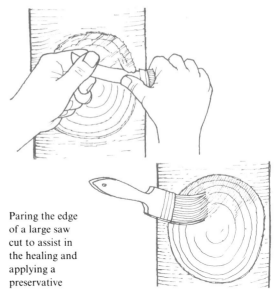

Paring the edge of a large saw cut to assist in the healing and applying a preservative

shoots which will carry next season's blooms.

The ever-popular cytisus should be lightly trimmed, removing approximately half the old flowering shoots. Shrub roses are a law unto themselves and I deal with mine in March. Any obviously dead or very old wood is cut clean out at the base. Then surplus or crossing branches are trimmed out and the bush generally tidied up.

Tree pruning is a dangerous undertaking requiring specialist knowledge. Having during over thirty-five years of gardening spent hours working many feet above ground level I speak from experience. Any limbs to be removed must be cut close to the trunk or the branch from which they spring. Indeed, this applies in all pruning; snags harbour pests and diseases which will ultimately destroy the host plant. Large branches should be under cut for at least a quarter of the way through which prevents ugly splintering of the stem. Better still take them down piecemeal by means of a rope, or call in a specialist who is properly insured. Dress all wounds with coal tar or a similar antifungicidal substance.

Suckers can be a problem particularly on grafted plants. Rhododendrons, lilacs, roses, some berberis, crabs and cherries are a few of the shrubs often worked on to a stock. Any growth from below soil level must be suspect and this is one good reason for avoiding deep digging near established shrubs, as this may cause damage to the roots which will lead to suckering. Unless I am certain the plants are not grafted such suckers are removed immediately, clearing away the soil to the point of origin, then pulling or cutting the unwanted growth away.

Standard trees, or trees with attractive stems, are treated with great care, any shoots which appear being removed while still small so no heavy cutting need be done.

Propagation

So much mystery and potting shed black magic has been woven into the work of propagation that the amateur, not surprisingly, makes a very tentative approach to the seedbox and propagating bench. Once the first inhibitions are lost there is a whole new fascinating field of gardening to be explored with possible attempts at hybridisation to evolve new varieties. One thing is absolutely certain, the seed or cutting is determined to grow whatever mistakes might be made by the propagator so at least there is a mutual interest straight away.

There is no need to spend vast sums on greenhouses and frames, or to put down acres to nursery beds. Usually only one or two plants are needed, one for the garden, the other to give away to a friend. A sheltered bed facing west or north, well provided with sand, will do fine for hardwood cuttings. There may be room to make a light sun frame which extends the range of semi-hardwood cuttings. Seed can be sown in pots, stood in the airing cupboard until germinated, then grown indoors until they are large enough to go outside. Nothing complicated, just a cheap, modest way of filling a garden with a large array of shrubs.

Seed. This is a feasible way of increasing stock when the plants concerned are species. Hybrids will not breed true from seed, so recourse must be made to cuttings, layers, budding, or grafting. The one big disadvantage of propagation by seed is the length of time which must elapse before a specimen is obtained of reasonable size for the shrub border. Open-ground sowing is usually only practised when a good stock of plants are needed i.e., when making a hedge or for screen planting. For holly, beech or hawthorn I use a narrow piece of garden sheltered by a beech hedge and get results which make the effort worthwhile. The bed must be well drained, and if the soil is at all heavy it will be necessary to work in a dressing of coarse sand. It must also be completely clear of weeds. Seed should be sown in the same type of soil as that favoured by the shrub or tree i.e., peaty soil for peat lovers, ordinary loamy soil for the great majority that will grow anywhere and so on.

Some seeds, mainly those contained inside berries and hips, need to go through a period of preparation known as stratification before they are sown. This simply means mixing the berries and hips, after they have been collected in the autumn, with sharp sand, then placing the mixture in a 5-in. pot and leaving it outside over winter. Care should be taken to label each species. Some fine zinc gauze should be placed over the top of the pot to prevent mice from eating the lot. The mixture will then freeze and thaw alternately throughout the winter and this treatment helps the flesh of the berries and hips to decay. In the spring the container can be emptied and the sand and seed sown in drills on the prepared bed where they will germinate quickly.

Depth of sowing depends very much on the type of seed. A good general rule is to cover them with soil to twice their own depth, but always wait until the soil is in a fine friable condition. Leave the seedlings undisturbed till they are several inches high and then transplant them at the normal planting season for the species, giving them ample room for further development. They can then be grown on for at least another year by which time they should be big enough to go out into their permanent quarters.

As interest grows the urge to try growing the less common, rather specialist shrubs from seed will make the purchase of a heated frame or greenhouse essential. I have never regretted purchasing my own small greenhouse; a pleasant retreat on cold or wet days with the initial price repaid in both plants and pleasure. A greenhouse will also be a valuable aid to rooting cuttings.

I always sow fine seed, like that of the rhododendrons, erica and kalmia, under glass where a careful watch can be kept on progress. A well-drained, aerated compost together with careful watering and controlled temperatures make success almost assured. Cleanliness of compost, of containers, of watering, and hygiene in general is an obvious requirement.

With rhododendrons I take a standard 4-in. seed-pan, fill it to $\frac{1}{3}$ of its depth with broken crocks and then add a thin layer of peat fibre which prevents the final material washing down to block the drainage. The final mixture, to within $\frac{1}{2}$ in. of the top, is made up of 2 parts sieved peat moss to 1 part of sand. Seed is sown very thinly and then firmed gently with a pot press. No covering of the compost is advisable or necessary. The pans are then covered with a sheet of glass which in turn is covered with a sheet of newspaper or brown paper to exclude light and prevent drying out. After germination the seedlings are shaded with muslin.

For less demanding shrubs the standard John Innes Seed Compost, made up of 2 parts loam, 1 part peat, and 1 sand will do very well. The loam is sterilised by heating it to about 82°C. or 180°F. to kill pests, weeds and diseases. To each bushel of the mixture add $1\frac{1}{2}$ oz. of superphosphate together with $\frac{3}{4}$ oz. of chalk. All the John Innes composts may be purchased ready for use from any garden shop or horticultural sundriesman. For those who prefer them, the no-soil composts based on peat are very good value.

Once the seedlings are large enough, prick them out into John Innes Potting Compost No.1. which is made up of 7 parts sterilised loam, 3 peat, 2 sand, plus $\frac{1}{4}$ lb. of John Innes base fertiliser, and $\frac{3}{4}$ oz. of chalk to each bushel of the mixture. John Innes base fertiliser is made up of $1\frac{1}{2}$ oz. of hoof and horn, $1\frac{1}{2}$ oz. of superphosphate and $\frac{3}{4}$ oz. of sulphate of potash. When seedlings have outgrown this second container they are normally big enough to go out into the open ground.

Cuttings. Most named varieties will only be

propagated true to type by means of vegetative propagation and cuttings or layers are the methods most frequently used. The cuttings of some species and varieties root with alacrity, for example the willow and forsythia, others need attention and persuasion.

Stem cuttings, in general, may be loosely grouped under three headings, softwood, semi-hardwood, and hardwood. No matter at what stage the cuttings are taken always dip them in a hormone rooting powder before insertion as this facilitates rooting considerably. Use a sharp knife so that the cut is clean which will help the base of the cutting to callous over quicker than a ragged tear. In fact, the best tool is a razor blade in a holder.

Only practical experience will teach the gardener how to select the best material, but some points are common sense. Cuttings are only taken from those shrubs which are true to variety, vigorous, and free from disease. They should also be taken from vegetative shoots and not those which end in a flower bud. They should be inserted into the rooting medium as soon as possible after being severed from the parent as there is then less risk of drying out. If for any reason this has to be delayed wrap the ends of the cuttings in moist cotton wool or sphagnum moss and put them in a polythene bag. This will keep them fresh for a short time.

Softwood cuttings are made from wood of current season's growth, before it has time to harden. They root very quickly but need careful handling as they are liable to dry out or fall prey to fungus disease. Ideally they should be 2 to 3 in. long, thin and short jointed. As with all cuttings remove the leaves from that part of the stem which is to go below soil level. These should be cut with a sharp razor blade and not pulled away as this damages the stem too much. It is important not to leave too many leaves on a cutting as these will increase the rate at which water is lost through transpiration which the cutting may be unable to make up, causing it to wither and die. At the same time the base can be trimmed back to immediately below the leaf joint making a nodal cutting. The majority of cuttings root most readily from this point, but there are exceptions which should be trimmed between the leaf joints to make internodal cuttings. As would be expected, the time of availability for softwood cuttings is late spring or early summer, i.e. May and early June.

Semi-hardwood cuttings are at a riper stage of growth than softwoods and are available from June into August. They can be either cut below a leaf joint, or pulled away with a piece of the old stem attached, or as professionals describe it with a heel of old wood. Although this is traditional it is not essential in most cases. An indication of ripeness for rooting is when the lower portion of the stem from which the cutting

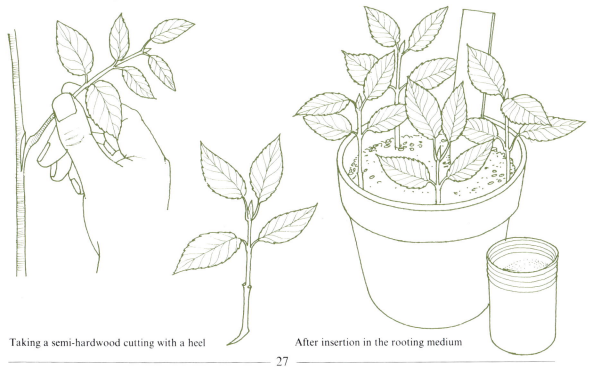

Taking a semi-hardwood cutting with a heel   After insertion in the rooting medium

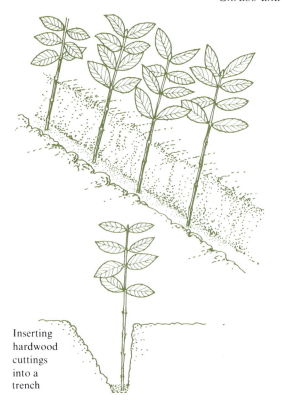

Inserting
hardwood
cuttings
into a
trench

is to be taken can be bent without breaking. An average length of 4 in. is what I would expect for this type of cutting, but as always there are exceptions, in particular heathers, which vouchsafe a niggardly $1\frac{1}{2}$ in.

A hardwood cutting is the best material for a raw beginner to make a first essay into the fascinating realms of plant propagation. These can be taken at leisure during the autumn and winter, whenever the weather is mild. They can be rooted either direct into the open border where they more or less look after themselves, apart from an occasional check to make sure the frost has not lifted them, or into a frame. Out of doors I have a narrow border only $2\frac{1}{2}$ ft. wide for ease of maintenance, which has served the purpose of a rooting nursery admirably for many years. As each bundle of cuttings is prepared, I take out a trench 4 to 6 in. deep, put a layer of sharp sand in the bottom, push the base of the cuttings well into this so there is no air space to inhibit rooting, then firm the soil back round the stems to the normal level. Over the years the soil has become very sandy and crisp and it improves season by season.

A cold frame need not be elaborate or very big and there are times when an orange box has served the purpose extremely well. To maintain the general appearance of the garden I prefer something neater made in wood, brick, breeze block, or cement. I use a two light frame, too big for cuttings really but it fills in for seedlings as well. The base is made up of 12 in. of broken brick to provide drainage and over this I put coarse ash and then the fine rooting medium. There are three internal divisions, one made up with sharp lime-free sand only, another with peat and sand in equal parts and the third with pumice. In this way I have a rooting medium to suit even the most fastidious cutting. For shading the cuttings during the first few critical weeks I use laths on nylon string, spaced 1 in. apart by pieces of polythene hosepipe. This frame is used mainly for soft, or semi-hardwood cuttings which need shading for the first fortnight. After this they can be fully exposed provided they are watered carefully. In hot weather this may be necessary three or four times a day.

When a greenhouse is available a corner can be reserved for a small propagating case; a small box 22 in. by 30 in., and 15 in. deep will hold a remarkable number of cuttings. For years I had such a box, the bottom made of asbestos which stood over a two burner paraffin heater. In this I rooted a host of shrubs from chamaecyparis to hebe, with never a moment's worry except to remember to fill the stove. Paraffin fumes have been known to kill some plants, my only losses occurred when the stove was turned up too high and spread foul black smoke over everything. Where electricity is available that chore can be removed by replacing the stove with soil-warming cables, controlled by means of a thermostat which keeps the rooting medium at exactly the required temperature. Handyman kits can be purchased or specialist-designed units can be bought.

Finally for the man who devotes all his time to the garden there is the mist unit bench. This automatically switches on a fine mist spray whenever the air surrounding the cuttings reaches a certain stage of dryness. This high degree of atmospheric humidity prevents the cuttings losing moisture and with thermostatically controlled soil warming providing an ideal rooting temperature the results achieved can be dramatic. Single atomising nozzle units are available at a reasonable price, together with a solenoid valve and an electronic leaf to switch it on and off. The system is not com-

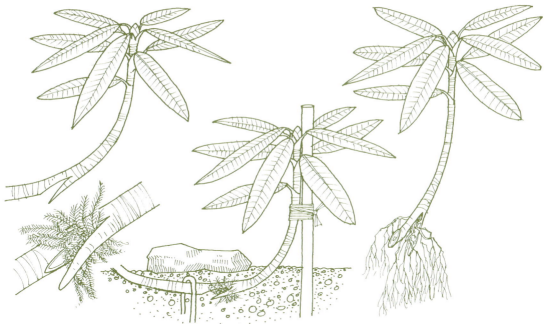

Layering

plicated to install or maintain and has proved better than 'green fingers' to the average gardener.

Where only a few cuttings are required which do not justify the expense of a small propagating unit, a polythene bag and a 5-in. pot will provide an alternative. I use pumice or sand as the rooting medium, filling the pot to within $\frac{1}{2}$ in. of the rim. Insert the cuttings around the edge of the pot, water, then put the whole thing inside the polythene bag which is then closed with a rubber band. In principle this is a facsimile of the closed, watertight frame, and works just as well.

Odd though it may seem there are shrubs which lend themselves with a little gentle persuasion to propagation by means of division, a perfectly legitimate short cut in my opinion for those possessed of sufficient confidence. In fact, when considering further plantings of romneya, pernettya, spiraea, even fuchsia, I lift existing plantings just as growth is starting in the spring and then with a spade filed really sharp, indulge in a little precise surgery, which reduces one plant to several healthy pieces. Replanted in soil prepared with sharp sand they quickly establish themselves and make flowering-sized specimens by the summer.

Layering. Most gardeners, especially those with a well-stocked garden do not want an endless series of young plants cluttering up the limited garden space. So far as most plants are concerned, layering is the easiest, surest and most labour-saving way of all to get vigorous young stock. So readily do some plants respond that wherever a branch touches the ground it roots. Not all are so obliging and must be helped in a small way. This process is known as layering and the main requirements are patience and a soil in good physical condition. A few weeks prior to layering work in a liberal quantity of peat and sharp sand around the selected plant. Any branches low enough to be pulled down to soil level will be suitable. At the point where the branch touches the soil make a cut of about 2 in. into the centre of the stem and then gently push a piece of sphagnum moss into the cut to hold it open. Peg the cut surface down firmly to the ground and cover with the sand-peat mixture to a depth of about 3 in. In addition to the peg and the layer of compost I place a large stone on top as this holds everything firm and keeps the compost underneath moist.

Where it is not possible to pull a branch down to soil level recourse may be made to the rather more difficult air-layering which has been brought within everyone's compass by the invention of polythene. I use this form of propagation for acers, certain rhododendrons, in fact anything rather special which may be reluctant to root from cuttings. The operation is carried out in April on young, disease-free wood of the previous season's growth. Remove a leaf

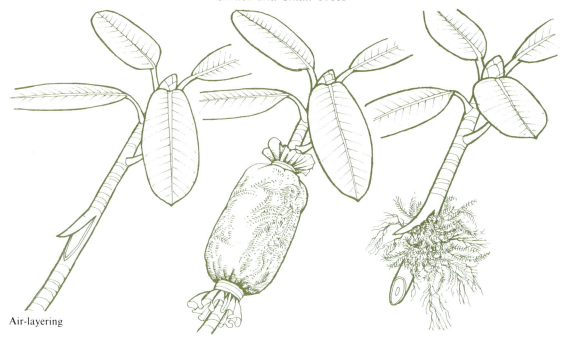

Air-layering

about 6 to 8 in. from the growing point. If it is any longer than this then the new plant, after it has been severed from the parent, will be difficult to re-establish. Make a cut half way through the stem beginning an inch below where the leaf was removed and continuing up to approximately half an inch above. Insert a twist of sphagnum moss to hold the cut open then paint the exposed surfaces with rooting powder. A polythene sleeve, made by slitting a suitably sized bag along the bottom, is then slipped over to enclose the wound and firmly bound at the base with electricians' tape. Pack moist sphagnum around the wound then seal the top of the bag. By moist I mean that a handful of the moss when squeezed just oozes water. To make certain the weakened stem does not break I tie the whole contraption firmly to a cane. Within eight to ten weeks in most cases roots will be seen spreading into the moss, and the new rooted portion can be cut away from the parent plant. I plunge all cuttings made like this into a compost of 1 loam, 1 peat, 1 sand, made up in a heavily shaded frame where there is no risk of them becoming dry until the white water roots establish themselves into a system capable of supporting the plant.

Budding and grafting. Eventually the keen gardener will want to try a few buds or grafts, and these are no more difficult than many other garden tasks. My first attempts at grafting resulted in one of my father's treasured James Grieve apple trees producing not only typical fruit but several branches of Laxtons as well. A sharp knife is of the utmost importance, indeed, the ability to maintain a keen edge on the blade makes the difference between success and failure. I prefer a straight blade and handle for all grafting work. The tying materials used are very much a matter of personal choice, but of the products available, a wide-ribboned soft raffia is my first choice. Grafting tape or ready-made ties are effective alternatives. Cold wax is less trouble to use than the limp wax which needs heating over a fire.

The stocks chosen for grafting are either lined out in nursery rows especially malus, prunus and pyrus, which can not be potted up, or, as with rhododendrons, peonies, conifers and similar ornamental shrubs, potted up into a cold house for working. For most forms of grafting the ideal situation is to have the stock in growth and the scion still dormant when the union is made. Of the 9 or 10 methods of grafting commonly practised in commercial horticulture, whip and tongue is the technique used more frequently than any other. To achieve a reasonable degree of success both the scion and rootstock sections to be married must be approximately the same size. This ensures that a large proportion of the cambium layer in both stock and scion is in intimate contact. The cambium is a thin layer of tissue composed during the growing season of actively dividing cells. Only these cells of both the scion and rootstock are capable of joining one to the other into an indissoluble whole.

Prepare the stock by cutting it down to the required height above soil level, for the beginner I would suggest 4 to 6 in. This should be done so that a sloping cut surface is left approximately $1\frac{1}{2}$ in. long. Finally a small downward cut is made half way up the slanting surface to leave a tongue. A matching cut is made on the scion to 'take a bud', or in simple terms a bud is left $\frac{1}{2}$ to $\frac{3}{4}$ of an inch from the tip, but on the opposite side to the cut surface. Then make a tongue to fit

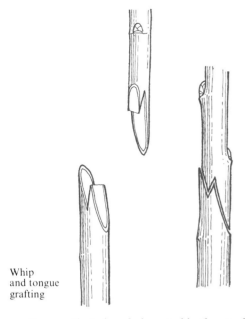

Whip
and tongue
grafting

neatly over that already inserted in the stock. Fit the two in position, see that the cambium layers are flush, bind them together with strips of moistened raffia, then paint the tie with grafting wax to complete an air and watertight seal.

Splice grafting is the same only without the tongue and I use it on soft-wooded clematis. Saddle grafting is used frequently for rhododendrons. *R. ponticum* stocks are grown on in pots on a warm bench for twelve months before working. At the appropriate season, as the sap lifts, make two slanting cuts on the scion in an upward direction to leave an inverted V like an old fashioned clothes peg. All that needs doing then is to shape the stock by making two similar slanting cuts at the top, leaving a saddle over which the scion can be seated. Bind these with raffia and plunge over a heated bench.

Budding is carried out during the growing season from late May to mid-September, when the bark lifts easily and ripe buds are available. The basic principles are the same so if the

enthusiast succeeds with roses he will soon graduate to cherries or any other ornamental shrub.

The rootstocks of roses are lined out the previous autumn. When selecting bud sticks look first at the shoots that have already flowered. The buds near the centre will usually prove ripe for insertion. Keep the sticks fresh after they are cut in moist sphagnum or a jar of water; first removing the leaves but leaving a small piece of stalk as a handle to hold the bud

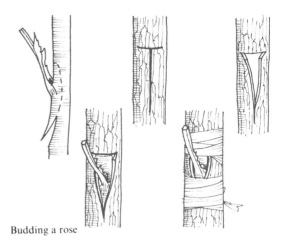

Budding a rose

while it is being inserted into the T cut.

Prepare the stocks for budding by clearing the soil away from around the base of the stem and wipe the exposed area clean with a moist cloth. Make a cross cut on the prepared surface, then an upward cut to meet it, drawing with the knife blade a letter T. The bark should lift easily with the knife handle if the stock is fit to bud. Remove the bud by starting a slanting cut one inch below the chosen bud and coming out the same distance above. The shield can be trimmed to size after insertion. A sliver of wood will be left behind the bud and this can be removed by bending it backwards and sideways. It is important to check that the core of the bud is not taken as well or the shell is useless. Open the T cut with the flattened end of the budding knife, slide the bud into position, trim the top level and the two flaps of bark should neatly embrace the shield. Bind the two flaps down with raffia or one of the ready-made ties now available, leaving the small portion of leaf stalk sticking out. If in due course this pulls away it is a good indication the bud has taken. Standard roses are budded in exactly the same way, except that the buds are inserted in the stem at

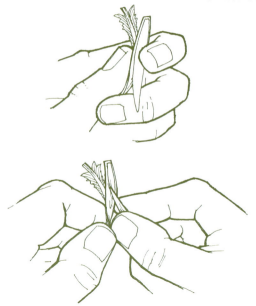

Removing the wood from behind the bud

anything from 3 to 6 ft. above the level of the soil.

Necessity is often the mother of invention, and certainly coveting a neighbour's cherry led me to my first attempt at budding. I had to walk past the tree of my desire every day on my way to work and in May it became a mass of tossed pink blossom against the blue and white of the Dales sky. After being promised bud wood I set about raising the stocks. The whole operation took three years because I grew the stocks from Morello cherry stones. These were chipped and grew prodigiously in moist sand. I prepared them for budding by removing all the side shoots for 15 in. above soil level. My father prepared the bud sticks by pinching out the growing tips in early June and I have since discovered that this plumps up the buds by ripening the wood.

My success with this first cherry, of four bud takes out of six tried, astonished the whole family.

The buds of ornamental trees and shrubs are made in the same way as for roses, starting an inch below the leaf stalk and emerging an inch above. Flowering crab apples do not mind if the slice of back wood is left but with cherries this must be removed. A quick flick with the knife blade is usually enough to free this sliver of wood but as with roses make sure the bud is not sent flying at the same time. Where the T-shaped cut is made depends on what type of tree is required. If a bush form is wanted then the cut is made 4 in. above soil level but with half or full standards from three to six feet of clean stem must be left. The bark is lifted, the bud inserted and bound exactly in the manner described for roses.

Keep the budded stocks clean weeded throughout the summer, then in the following March head back the stem to 3 or 4 in. above the bud. In due course the buds which were inserted will begin to grow, and when the shoots are large enough they can be tied to the snag left above them – a practice which prevents them being broken off by birds or wind. Any suckers which appear, as they inevitably seem to, should be removed before they make too much growth. All the available food will be sent up to the terminal buds so that by October the snag of old wood to which the shoot was tied can be cut away.

Rootstocks for crataegus, sorbus, laburnum, and many other trees can be raised so easily from berries gathered from fields and woodland that budding and grafting offer a cheap, albeit fascinating, method of furnishing the garden.

Hedging Plants

Inevitably, with the increase in population, the demand for buildings to house it, and the limited supply of that priceless commodity land, gardens must get smaller. Though a hedge around the outer periphery reduces the garden area still further, the desire for privacy is sufficient reason for most people to plant a screen of some sort. In common with most enthusiasts I love to invite people to see my plants yet I still feel justified in demanding a degree of seclusion to enjoy my flowers and the labour of growing them. The shrubs chosen for hedging must be beautiful in their own right, either in leaf, berry, or flower, hardy enough to stand the rigours of soil or climate, and thick enough to give shelter without constant attention. The list of shrubs which approach this standard of excellence is surprisingly long.

An evergreen hedge will supply the maximum amount of protection because the foliage is retained throughout the full twelve months of the year. A well-tended hedge of chamaecyparis provides excellent shelter and a pleasant relief to the eye in a mainly deciduous landscape. A deciduous hedge will be cheaper to buy initially and in most cases easier to establish. Whatever the hedge chosen cultivations before planting are the same.

The site must be deeply worked with a plentiful dressing of organic matter and should then be allowed to stand over winter. In late February, as the soil dries out, work in a dressing of a complete fertiliser at 2 oz. per sq. yd., then allow a further fortnight for the soil to settle and begin planting. If the land tends to hang a little wet, raise the centre somewhat above the surrounding area. However, if there is a positive waterlogging a proper drainage system is the only solution. The spacing of the individual plants will depend on the genus and species being used but if this distance is to be anything up to 18 in. apart take out a trench. Above this distance individual holes are less labour. Sometimes when a thicker hedge is needed quickly a system of double row planting can be adopted with the plants in the second row being planted between those in the first row.

The arguments as to the season for planting rage perennially in gardening circles but given the choice I prefer mid-March. Once planted make sure the shrubs do not dry out and if necessary water twice a day. A thick mulch of peat ensures that the soil retains a comfortable amount of moisture, having first made sure that the roots were well soaked before they went under ground. Most hedges grow at a rate which permits the roots to balance and support the top growth, unless very large specimens are used and this practice is fraught with all sorts of perils. One hedge which grows so quickly it does need staking for the first five years until pruning restores the balance is *Cupressocyparis leylandii*. Rather than stake individuals I put up a single

Escallonia x *langleyensis*

Berberis darwinii is a thoroughly reliable evergreen shrub. The orange-yellow flowers are followed by purple fruits. This shrub is tolerant enough of pruning to be used for hedging.

The rich red-purple foliage of *Berberis thunbergii atropurpurea* is invaluable as an accent point in the shrub border. The naturally upright habit and tolerance of clipping make this berberis a useful shrub for hedging purposes.

The Lawson Cypress
has produced numerous
cultivars, many small
enough to plant in the
rock garden while
others grow into speci-
men trees. *Chamaecy-
paris lawsoniana*
Triomphe de Boskoop
is just one of many
varieties which can be
grown as a hedge.

Though escallonia are a
feature of coastal
gardens they will grow
and flower well inland
provided they are given
a place in full sun.
Apple Blossom is a
pink and white flowered
variety.

rail fence 36 in. high and the bushes support themselves as they grow round it.

Opinions vary as to when pruning or clipping should commence and this does depend very much on the type of plant, exposure, and state of growth. Hawthorn is usually cut hard back after one year to almost soil level whereas I let beech run for five years at least, only trimming the sides but not the top. The subsequent cultivations include controlling weeds, watching for pests and diseases, an annual feed of a balanced fertiliser and renewal of the mulch as it is broken down into the soil.

Evergreen hedges

Almost any shrub which will stand a modest pruning can be persuaded into making a hedge but these do not concern us here for they are at best limited in scope, at worst a shocking waste of effort. The evergreen berberis contain several species which have proved perfectly amenable to restraint. The two best known are *Berberis darwinii* and *B*. x *stenophylla,* both shrubs of real quality in form and flower. If *B. darwinii,* a native of Chile, is given regular attention to clipping it will eventually make a dark green barrier 6 ft. in height which in April – May is glorious in bright orange flower. Unless clipped each year after flowering, however, the lower branches die out to leave the base embarrassingly naked. This berberis can be planted at anything between 2 and 3 ft. apart. *B*. x *stenophylla* is only suitable where space is available for the shrub to develop in full its long arching branches which are wreathed in April with deep yellow fragrant flowers. Clipped immediately after flowering it will grow up to 8 ft. in height and as much through and it does not resent hard pruning if it exceeds the allotted space. I plant at 36 in. apart, the suckering habit soon fills the gap. *B. gagnepainii* and *B. verruculosa* are both worthy of consideration if a neat, compact barrier will suffice.

I suffered *Buxus sempervirens* for seven years around what seemed to me, as a teenager, endless miles of border to be clipped, cleaned, rescued from snow, in fact, wet nursed to distraction. My opinion is, therefore, clouded by torment endured. In a town garden or a shady site box could be pressed into service, but enough, I malign a plant which has done yeoman service. Regular feeding and clipping are essential or the bushes become bare and leggy.

Of the cotoneaster, a genus which includes so many beautiful shrubs, only one has proved of outstanding value for hedging purposes. *Cotoneaster simonsii* is really neither evergreen nor deciduous so it was difficult to decide which section it should come under. Strange that a shrub so fiercely upright in habit should reflect an air of informality. In autumn every twig of its 6-ft. frame is festooned with orange-scarlet berries, a spectacle enhanced by some of the leaves remaining green while others take on the full panoply of autumn scarlet. Plant at 18 to 24 in. apart and trim in February.

Chamaecyparis lawsoniana is frequently used as a large untrimmed screen and it is especially effective in a large garden which is sheltered from strong winds. For the smaller garden, one of the selected named varieties would be suitable. These give uniform growth up to a correctly anticipated height. The best I have tried so far is Green Hedger, a closely branched erect bush with deep green foliage. After 7 years this variety has reached 6 ft. in height in my own garden without spreading far enough to need clipping. Spacing should be 3 ft. apart, unless money is no object when they could go in at 2 ft. apart making a solid barrier quicker but serving no other useful purpose. Both *C. l. fletcheri* and *C. l. fraseri* have quietly attractive grey-green leaves growing to about 12 ft. high in the fullness of time. A mixture of the green forms with the yellow-foliaged *stewartii* or *smithii* makes a picturesque screen on a sheltered site.

Cupressocyparis leylandii has played an important part in sheltering the vulnerable herbaceous plants delphiniums, lupins and peonies on an exposed hillside here in Harrogate. Considering it was discovered almost a century

Buxus sempervirens

ago it has taken many years to be recognised for what it is, namely a top-class hedging plant. In 5 or 6 years it will make a well-furnished barrier 9 to 10 ft. high and it will readily respond to being clipped twice a year. Plant at $2\frac{1}{2}$ to 3 ft. apart. If cuttings are required, in my experience these should be taken in February and rooted in a propagating frame. Stake the plants as previously described with a single rail fence 36 in. high.

Ilex aquifolium, the ever-popular holly known from childhood with the polished evergreen leaves and scarlet berries, makes a picture I love to see, providing it is in someone else's garden! There are several groups of ilex in my boundary hedge, and a proportion of the leaves shed in July make weeding a painful business. Clip in July or when required; plant at anything from 18 to 30 in. apart or mix with crataegus in the ratio of 3 holly to 5 hawthorn.

Ligustrum ovalifolium aureum

Ligustrum ovalifolium, Oval-leaf Privet, and the golden-leaved form *aureum* have for many years served cities the length and breadth of the British Isles, and it is perhaps for this reason that we tend to treat what is in reality a useful plant with indifference bordering on contempt. In almost any conditions from calcareous clay to acid sand it exhibits a serene good temper. For single rows space the plants at 12 in. apart, for double rows 12 to 18 in. staggered, with 12 in. between the rows. Individuals should be cut back hard the first year to make them branch from the base.

Lonicera nitida must have had the best public relations officer ever, for during the golden era of gardening it was overplanted to an extent which bordered on the ridiculous. Most of the gardens I visit seem to have at least one overgrown, neglected lonicera hedge, even if only as a screen to the compost heap. Carefully tended with fortnightly clippings it is a good hedging plant, but I would never again plant lonicera. For seven years I slaved over a hedge 70 ft. long then, just as it seemed my labours would be rewarded, a heavy fall of snow spread it over about 9 ft. of garden, a liberty from which it never recovered. Space the young plants at 12-in. intervals and cut hard back in March – April. Cuttings root with nonchalent ease at any time during the growing season.

I have always had a great admiration for *Taxus baccata* both as a hedge and specimen tree. Unfortunately, even using large transplants, many years must pass before we can sit in the shade of a yew planted by our own hands. Under no circumstances should yew be planted where grazing animals can reach it or there could be tragic repercussions for the whole tree is poisonous – wood, leaves and berries. People who already possess a yew hedge should clip, feed, and cherish it, lavishing on it the care usually reserved for the family heirloom. Individuals should be spaced at $1\frac{1}{2}$ to 2 ft. apart although in times of financial embarrassment I have stretched this to $2\frac{1}{2}$ ft.

Both *Griselinia littoralis* and *Laurus nobilis* make impressively beautiful foliaged hedges in favoured areas. Indeed, when grown in a suitable climate griselinia will accept any soil or aspect, even growing under oak trees. Plant the griselinia $1\frac{1}{2}$ to 2 ft. apart, the *Laurus nobilis* at 2 ft. Trim as required during the growing season.

The first house I lived in was called The Laurels for the obvious reason that the whole front garden was enclosed by an immense hedge of Cherry Laurel, *Prunus laurocerasus,* 6 ft. high and 8 ft. thick. The hours spent searching for cricket balls in the stygian gloom of this handsome shrub could have been better spent learning the art of that most noble game itself. The bushes were planted 36 in. apart but this could be reduced to 24 in. to achieve a quicker coverage. Trim in the first years with secateurs, then ignoring the fact that some of the foliage effect is lost trim the bushes with shears in May or July.

On acid soils *Rhododendron ponticum* will make a labour-saving barrier, but tends to be rather slow growing. The spacing is 24 to 36 in.

The Purple Beech, *Fagus sylvatica purpurea*, makes an efficient, easily maintained and ornamental hedge. A tapestry of colour from spring to autumn and beautiful even in winter, for the russet dead leaves are retained until spring before being shed.

A hedge of *Fuchsia magellanica riccartonii* is ornamental rather than functional. Grown as a shrub in the garden the long flowering season can be properly appreciated.

Ilex aquifolium aureo-marginata is really a collective name for varieties with gold-edged leaves. I prefer the berrying females which make superb specimen plants and are also useful for a boundary hedge.

The Oregon Grape, *Mahonia aquifolium*, makes an effective hedge. The clustered racemes of rich yellow flowers persist for several weeks in early spring and are followed, in due course, by blue-black berries.

Prunus lusitanica

Berberis thunbergii atropurpurea

There are, of course, other evergreens which make hedges. *Prunus lusitanica* with dark rich green leaves is very good. Two others worthy of consideration would be the pyracantha, though this can be expensive, or rosemary, *Rosmarinus officinalis*, especially on a warm well-drained soil. Both rosemary and lavender may be used to divide the garden but are ineffectual as boundary hedges. They may both be spaced at 18 in. apart and will, with regular clipping, make beautiful assets to the garden.

Deciduous Hedges

Again the choice is bewildering, but I shall simplify the list, restricting my choice to only the outstandingly good, rather than the average. *Berberis thunbergii* and the red-foliaged form *atropurpurea* are so close growing they need hardly any trimming. The autumn colour is brilliant and a mixture of 5 red and 3 green, makes a garden feature of considerable merit. I plant at 18 in. apart but 24 in. is usually recommended.

Carpinus betulus, the hornbeam, is a majestic fluted column of a tree growing free and unrestricted, yet capable of being persuaded into the clipped uniformity of a hedge. Unlike the beech it does not retain the dead leaves over winter, but in every other respect it is practically identical. In single rows the young plants go out at 12 to 15 in. apart.

A mixture of hornbeam and the hawthorn (crataegus) makes a most attractive boundary to the garden, or instead of the hornbeam, substitute holly to make a barrier which would deter even apple-hungry young boys. The common thorn is cheap, readily obtainable, tolerant of clipping even when old, and will grow in most soils. Seed stratified over winter in sand offers an easy

Prunus laurocerasus

Forsythia

Penzance Briar rose

means of raising stock. The youngsters are ready for the final move after 2 years, being headed hard back the first winter after planting. Space at 12 in. apart and keep trimmed fairly hard to encourage dense growth.

Of all the hedges, the common beech, *Fagus sylvatica*, did the most to make gardening tolerable on the wickedly exposed site at Harlow Car. Perhaps its one fault was that the leaves, retained during the winter, were usually shed just when all my attention had to be concentrated on seed sowing and the other delights of spring. Contrary to popular belief the beech is tolerant of a wide range of soils including this heavy clay of mine. I do not clip for the first few years, with the possible exception of shortening back the longer side branches, but just let the hedge make height without discouragement. Plant at 12 to 18 in. apart. If coloured varieties are required 5 purple or copper to 3 green is about the right proportion.

Some years ago, eleven to be precise, I was given three or four different 'plum' hedges to try. *Prunus cerasifera atropurpurea,* mixed in the proportion of 2 to 1 with East Malling Myrobalan B, was one. The former has purple leaves, the latter green and the contrast is exceptionally fine. Planted at 1½ ft. apart, I was content to sit and watch them grow but two years later the

gentleman who gave them to me descended on the garden with heavy pruners and cut the lot down to ground level. There is now a superb hedge, thick, strong and some 5 ft. high. Clipped once or sometimes twice a year it gives no trouble.

Prunus cistena has a leaf which in sunlight glows deep scarlet and spaced at 12 in. apart it makes a fine dwarf hedge to top a retaining wall or terrace. The blossom and scarlet growth make this small shrub a special favourite of mine though, no doubt, the excellent colour is in part due to the fact that I spoil it with extra feeding and mulching.

Some roses make colourful hedges, but I have seen few preserve the neatness essential in a small garden, or if they did then there were no flowers. There is a Penzance Briar hedge at the bottom of the garden, a mixture of several named varieties and though it takes up rather a lot of space when all the branches are festooned with pink or dark red flowers, not an inch of garden is missed.

Zéphirine Drouhin, given the support of a trellis, makes a neat barrier. The sweetly scented pink flowers open in succession from June until November, sometimes after if the weather stays mild. Musk roses like Penelope, Felicia, and Cornelia offer the same colourful

The Portugal Laurel, *Prunus lusitanica*, will make a specimen ever-green tree when un-pruned, but can also be clipped to form a hedge.

Though *Pyracantha watereri* can be trimmed to form a hedge, heavier crops of bright red fruits are produced when this hybrid is allowed to grow unrestricted.

Roses make colourful hedges especially if a mixture of several varieties is used. They do take up rather a lot of space, however, and should be positioned with care.

Few people who plant a yew live long enough to rejoice in its mature shade. The Golden-leaved Yew, *Taxus baccata aurea*, though slow growing is, even in youth, a quality foliage plant which also makes an attractive hedge.

response. Many of the taller floribundas – Heidelberg, Fred Loads, Dainty Maid or Queen Elizabeth make hedges of a sort, but if correctly pruned provide no barrier for three months of the year, and have an average life of about 12 years only, unless carefully fed.

The shrubs listed would be my first choice but an inexpensive hedge may be obtained simply by the effort of pushing prunings from forsythia and *Ribes sanguineum* into a trench lined with sharp sand. These root very quickly as I discovered when using them as supports for my early peas. When rooted, plant up in the ratio of three forsythia to two ribes, spacing the individual plants 18 in. apart. Prune with secateurs immediately after flowering until the hedge is established, then the trimming may be done with shears.

Escallonia will make a most attractive hedge which is deciduous in cold inland gardens and evergreen in coastal areas. When I was gardening in Cornwall, bushes spaced at 24 in. apart thickened to a fine barrier in 4 years, whereas at Harlow Car garden 18 in. proved the most suitable distance to leave individuals. There are several good hybrids from which a choice can be made including C. F. Ball, crimson, good in coastal areas; Donard Radiance, rose red, more compact in habit; Donard Seedling, pink fading to white, very good at Harlow Car, up to 8 ft. high; *edinensis,* shell pink, an old favourite, up to 6 ft. high; and *langleyensis,* deep pink, about 6 ft.

Some of the taller growing heathers make neat informal hedges. I am thinking in particular of *Erica terminalis* which grows 3 ft. or rather more in height and in winter, if left untrimmed, has a pleasant russet and green appearance as the faded flower heads are retained until spring. I allow 18 in. between individual specimens in the hedge. Trimming may be done immediately after the pink flowers fade in July or left, as I do, until March. This is a heath which will tolerate a certain amount of lime in the soil.

Another shrub which will make a most effective low flowering hedge, even in fairly shady conditions, is the Oregon Grape, *Mahonia aquifolium*. I discovered this more or less by accident when having some 20 to 30 rooted cuttings to spare I heeled them in on a rough bank which bounded one side of the orchard at Hurworth, County Durham. Though shaded by walnut and cherry the cuttings grew into a dark green barrier which was lovely in flower during April but equally attractive when festooned with blue-black berries later in the year. During autumn a percentage of the foliage turns deep red while the remainder maintains the evergreen habit.

Ground Cover Plants

A great deal has been said and written about ground cover plants, much of which, on analysis, seems to assume a Utopian condition of soil and climate which is beyond my present experience. When such plants develop sufficient foliage to smother weeds, as they must to be functional, they make mulching or feeding in any other form than liquid well nigh impossible. Good ground cover plants must, therefore, be tolerant of a certain amount of shade and root competition, while still growing strongly enough to smother any weeds at birth. I would rather go through a shrub border devoid of ground cover with a hoe than try to clean a border, supposedly labour saving, in which the weeds and plants fight a battle for supremacy.

With a two-tier vegetation system the soil must be in the best physical condition before any planting is done, remembering that there will be two root systems to feed. In addition, and this is a very important point, the land must be free of any perennial weeds. Very few shrubs I know will smother out established bindweed or ground elder. They are even capable of competing with the all-conquering heather.

As the garden grows to maturity there will be more areas of bare earth beneath the taller shrubs and standard trees. This is not a new problem for in a catalogue printed in 1905 there is a list of plants for growing under trees. Care should be exercised or the weed suppressor may in turn become the weed as not infrequently happens with some of the rampant bamboos.

However, I have probably given the impression that the term ground cover is limited to those areas already planted with shrubs which need a mulch of plants to cover the weeds. This would be incorrect. Ground cover plants can be used anywhere in the garden on dry sloping banks, in shade, to disguise manhole covers – in fact wherever a mask of greenery is required.

The heather garden can be left for weeks on end with very little attention and yet still present an air of respectability in all but the wettest seasons. Some find them dull and uninteresting but I find their infinite variety, long flowering season, and ability to withstand all degrees of exposure a heaven-sent gift to gardeners, like myself, who have a windswept site to cultivate. Once the plants cover the ground few weeds can

Varieties of *Hedera helix*

The arching wide-spreading branches of *Cotoneaster conspicuus* are ideal for covering steep banks, hiding man-hole covers or for providing a contrast in shape in the shrub border.

Hypericum calycinum, the ubiquitous Rose of Sharon is an adaptable, if invasive, ground cover for sun or shade. The 18-inch high evergreen canopy is a perfect foil to the golden yellow flowers.

OPPOSITE
The berries of *Pernettya mucronata* will excite comment throughout the winter until the first flowers appear in June.

Erica x *darleyensis*

Erica mediterranea

Erica carnea King George

successfully penetrate the blanket of vegetation. An acid soil is essential if all the heathers both erica and calluna are to survive. On an alkaline soil plantings must be confined to varieties of *Erica carnea, E. terminalis* and *E.* x *darleyensis* and certain Mediterranean varieties which are to a degree lime tolerant, providing the alkalinity is not excessive. My reason for the proviso is that *Erica* Arthur Johnson looked very sick when I planted it in limestone chips, if a bilious shade of yellow is any indication of ill health. A mistake I once made was to plant a part of the garden with heathers before putting in the impact plants, conifers, kalmia, acers, and others to give a change of foliage texture. Now I plant the bones so to speak only after infinite thought, then it is easy to group the erica and calluna around them.

With care, a well-composed heath garden will be colourful for most months of the year either in flower or foliage. I mulch with peat until growth makes this impracticable, and trim back those plants which obviously need restraint about every 2 years, after they have flowered.

Not surprisingly the *ericaceae* offers another genus with members which make as good and in some respects better weed suppressors than the heathers. In rhododendrons the gardener finds the most colourful of all evergreens with beautiful flowers and in some cases striking foliage and form. There is one weakness in this near paragon of a plant's versatility, it abhors lime in any shape or form, so can only be grown in acid soil. I like to see rhododendrons planted in open woodland, for they are shrubs which lend themselves, with charm, to the informal type of gardening. Once planted and established the evergreen varieties cast such a dense shade that this, together with a network of surface roots, is usually enough to discourage the most enterprising weed.

As a confirmed rhododendron devotee I tend towards species or hybrids with good foliage as the leaves are always with us, the flowers being a welcome bonus for a season before I return to a grateful contemplation of contrasting greens. For those who have a woodland corner about 40 ft. × 20 ft. I would suggest a grouping which for many years has given me pleasure beyond mere words to describe. First *Rhododendron wightii* which has deep green foliage with fawn underside and flowers of pale yellow splashed scarlet. Then add a centrepiece of two

R. bureavii with leaves dark green above and rusty red underneath, and one *R. smirnowii* making a perfect contrast having leaves grey on top and white below. For a long time I debated what species to include in the remaining corner, and decided it had to be my favourite *R. thomsonii* with beautiful metallic-grey foliage and superb wax-red flowers. For the last 15 years the bed has had, or needed, very little attention.

Prostrate conifers offer great fields of exploration to the enquiring mind, endless permutations for the mathematically inclined. I have only briefly investigated the possibilities but have been sufficiently gratified by my initial experiments to try many more. For three years a corner of a path in the rock garden resisted all my best efforts to keep it neat until in exasperation I put in a *Juniperus sabina tamariscifolia*. Slowly the canopy of pale green has spread to cover all the aridity of weed-ridden stone. Now the plant is 48 in. across but barely 12 in. high.

Most people who become enamoured of a rock garden learn by their mistakes. My initial efforts could be described as a series of catastrophies. Fortunately I had the good sense to plant most of the rock pile with conifers, and now it passes all but the closest examination. *Juniperus communis prostrata* and the fascinating Waukegan Juniper, *J. horizontalis douglasii,* whose silver-blue branches change to plum purple in winter, have contributed greatly to the transformation. To provide colour contrast I have included one golden-leaved *J.* x *media plumosa aurea.*

This low-growing shrub colony is added to whenever another nursery is visited. I feel much sympathy for wives of people like myself who find it impossible to pass a nursery without going in to browse. From Winchester, Hampshire, I had two fine *Cotoneaster adpressus praecox,* a strong growing yet prostrate variety with large orange berries and a first-class weed and, if given the chance, plant smotherer for its enthusiasm knows no bounds. Bolton by Bowland, Yorkshire, provided *Cotoneaster congestus*, a creeping evergreen gem following every configuration of the ground. To encourage hummock formation which adds interest, I put down one or two stones for the stems to arch over. A *Genista pilosa* and *Rhododendron impeditum,* the former with yellow and the latter with blue flowers, complete the picture. While the plants were growing in, the bare earth was covered with a 2-in. layer of granite chippings to discourage weeds, and for several years now a weed has been a cause for comment.

Cherries are a magnificent spectacle in full flower against a May sky, and two in particular give me immense pleasure, framing as they do an expanding view of the dale beyond. Until recently the bare earth underneath resisted all my efforts to cover its nakedness, until I was presented with a collection of vinca. Not wishing to have more deaths on my conscience I covered the bed with 6 in. of compost before planting, and only regular mowing has stopped the hard polished wave of green spreading into the lawn. Flowers in blue, purple and white make a pleasant undertone to summer, but I prefer the vinca when all its polished leaves are starred with spent cherry blossom.

As a raw beginner I believed all that was written in books, and in most cases this was perfectly satisfactory as experience proved. There are occasions, however, when what is right for the South is wrong for the North. A case in point would be pernettya and gaultheria which for years I did not realise could produce more than a modest half dozen berries. Eventually I tried a bed of *Gaultheria miqueliana* and *Pernettya mucronata* Bell's Seedling on a steeply sloping, rather dry bank which received a fair share of sun and the results astonished me. The 12-in. high hummocks of gaultheria disappeared under a mass of white berries. Even more surprising was the pernettya whose branches arched over with the weight of red fruit which persisted until the flowers opened the following May.

Viburnum davidii remains a neat compact shrub on my clay soil and has the most attractive dark green leaves which are especially valuable in winter. I grew the plant for 10 years before discovering that unless male and female are present there are no bright blue berries to lighten the October days. I immediately stopped condemning our bees, bought three male viburnums and have had berries on the female ever since. The looser growth of the male does permit the odd weed to invade but they are worth the five minutes work necessary to remove them.

Some hebes have proved splendid material, especially under shrub roses, in my garden. *Hebe buxifolia* was the first I tried around and under *Rosa* Nevada. In due season the planting matured and now the hebe, only 15 in. high, makes a splendid background to the white flowers of

Once established, heathers make weed suppressors which are only surpassed by a 2-in layer of concrete. Silver birch provide the ideal silhouette background to this heather garden.

The multitudinous varieties of our common ling have a special place in my affection. I have only to look at this illustration to feel a sense of isolation only apparent when walking alone on the heather-covered moors. Unfortunately none of the varieties will tolerate any but an acid soil.

The value of contrasting foliage and shapes is so often underestimated. Here
dwarf conifers and others are used to delightful effect.

Nevada. *H. buchananii* performs a similar function underneath another lovely rose, the pale yellow Agnes.

Shrubs capable of being clipped do present possibilities for under planting. I was impressed by a garden in the Lake District where the drive to the front door was lined on either side with sycamores most effectively carpeted with common laurel, hard pruned to 18 in., making a solid boskage of bright green leaves.

A small prostrate yew, *Taxus baccata horizontalis*, performs a similar function under a solitary Field Maple on the lane border in this garden. Strange that it took a friendly visitor's appreciation to draw my attention to the service the native Blaeberry, *Vaccinium myrtillus*, gives as sub-scrub in the woodland. Cut with a rotary grass cutter as it becomes over grown it makes a thoroughly pleasant weed-free carpet, and the berries attract many birds which give further interest.

Naturally plants which are very shade tolerant are most useful and I have on several occasions had reason to be grateful for *Daphne laureola* in this respect. Now when a labour-saving border is needed, I try one group of the daphne as the leaves are attractive though the insignificant yellow flowers are but a fleeting nonentity.

I once saw *Skimmia laureola* in a shady bed when visiting a garden and while stepping over it I accidentally crushed some leaves only to discover they have a pungent though not unpleasant aroma.

The varieties of *Hedera helix* make a pleasant evergreen carpet under deciduous trees and shrubs, especially if the handsome foliage is enlivened here and there with groups of snowdrops or narcissus.

The gallant Rose of Sharon, *Hypericum calycinum*, saved me endless work by condescending to clothe the sides of a dry shady bank, surmounted by standard prunus trees which had been a constant source of irritation for years. Though my admiration is undimmed, experience with the same plant has caused me to be grateful that in this my first experiment it was confined from spreading beyond a prescribed limit by a flagstone path set in concrete. However, the large yellow flowers are sufficient compensation for the small labour of clipping the old shoots hard back each spring.

Like many professional gardeners I enjoy being shown around other gardens as frequently

I see in them plantings which can be reproduced in my own garden. I first saw *Phillyrea angustifolia* growing under a magnolia in a garden called Silver Wood which is situated near to Alnwick, Northumberland. To my mind this is a near-perfect woodland garden. The narrow dark evergreen leaves of the phillyrea with the enormous cups of *Magnolia* x *soulangiana* flowers towering above made an indelible impression. Needless to say, I tried the same scheme here and must patiently await the result.

Ignorance can sometimes be a blessing. For many years I grew *Lithospermum diffusum* without the slightest trouble. The cuttings rooted with vulgar alacrity and I honoured this beautiful shrub by poking a specimen of it in wherever space permitted. To prevent primulas seeding under some shrubs growing only a path's width away I carpeted the soil beneath the shrubs with *Lithospermum* Heavenly Blue. The mat of leaves was covered with a mass of blue flowers in early summer. Indeed, these continued intermittently until the autumn. Then I read that this plant is difficult to root and started to take extra care with the cuttings. I lost all but three from one batch so that now I continue my old practice and once again the cuttings root with perfect composure and no difficulty.

The growth of the Butcher's Broom, *Ruscus aculeatus*, is closely packed, and the spine-tipped leaves appear highly polished as if they were varnished. Though extremely shade tolerant it resents a very wet acid soil, and berries sparsely in poor light conditions. Only once, in Northumberland, have I seen the bright red marble fruits really thick on a bush which was sited on the west face of a low wall.

For me the appreciation of the beauties of *Colchicum speciosum album* was over shadowed by the thought of its unsightly leaves in spring until I used a *Cotinus coggygria foliis purpureis* as ground cover to the bulbs. Each spring I hard prune the shrub and the colchicum leaves develop then die to be hidden by the bright purple leaves of the rhus. In autumn the pure white goblet flowers of the colchicum look superb against the autumn glory of the rhus. A desperate measure has proved a delightful remedy.

From a plant with such a hardy constitution as the potentilla one would naturally expect additional virtues, and I have certainly taken liberties with this genus which only the best

Ruscus aculeatus

natured would endure. So far the happiest marriage was when I used the Purple-leaved Sand Cherry, *Prunus* Crimson Dwarf *(cistena)* with *Potentilla* Longacre. The first named grows 24 in. high, has bright purple leaves with pink flowers, and can be hard clipped. The potentilla grows 18 in. high and has yellow flowers throughout summer and autumn. The resulting thicket permits no weeds to grow and is altogether lovely. I have no doubt there are other shrubby cinquefoils which could be substituted for the variety Longacre. In my own experience *beanii*, Elizabeth and *fruticosa mandshurica (glabra mandshurica)* show a similar weed smother aptitude.

For several years I had the greatest difficulty

Cotinus coggygria foliis purpureis

in persuading *Kalmia latifolia* to grow until, more by accident than anything else, I underplanted it with *Mahonia aquifolium*. The kalmia grows and flowers above a blanket of dark green leaves. In spring the mahonia is magnificent with racemes of rich yellow, sweetly scented flowers, followed by black berries and though evergreen some of the leaves turn scarlet. I am not sure if it is the root shade or the protection the underplanting affords, but both the kalmia and the garden are better served by the insertion of the mahonia. The other ground hugging mahonia, *M. repens rotundifolia*, will thrive in most soils except where drainage is bad. In the winter garden it will soon smother the bare earth. I grow it under *Viburnum* x *bodnantense*.

Six years ago I was given a shrub from a vicarage garden which was new to me, but it had the habit of growth which indicated it would make suitable ground cover. It has made a perfect underplanting to forsythia, having grown only 18 in. high by about 6 ft. across, with bright green leaves and rather nondescript flowers which are followed by attractive purple berries. After considerable investigation I found out that it is a form of *Lonicera pileata*, and as the branches are self layering I am now using it in other parts of the garden, particularly as a foliage contrast in association with heathers.

By judicious mixing of deciduous with evergreen shrubs, it is possible to achieve not only the most effective foliage contrasts but also reduce the labour required to maintain a border in good order to negligible proportions. But be warned! Unless the soil is in first-class condition

A happy blend of rock, plant and water which will add an extra dimension to the garden scene. *Cytisus kewensis* is the attractive cream shrub.

Azaleas and heathers harmonise in this lovely woodland garden to express a sense
of peace in marked contrast to the changing world outside.

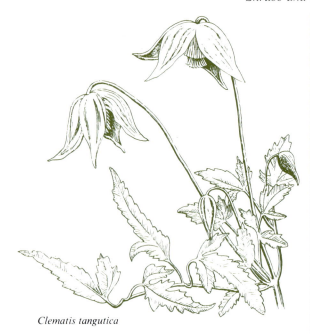

Clematis tangutica

before planting is begun only a very tatter-demalion-like effect will result.

The smaller garden requires a sympathetically judicious use of weed-suppressing shrubs otherwise, if outrageously invasive plants are used, it quickly becomes a monoculture. A friend of mine once planted snowberry under laburnum and flowering crabs across the boundary to his garden. Eventually he gave up the struggle to keep the suckering roots of the symphoricarpos within bounds, and built a hen run on that piece of land instead.

I have a problem corner in my own garden which after fourteen years of experiment has achieved a harmony which makes it one of the most pleasant beds in the garden. If one shrub failed to impress or permitted that pernicious

weed landcress to survive it was removed and another was acquired from elsewhere in the garden. Now for much of the year it is quietly lovely, especially in spring time. There are five dwarf rhododendrons which grow only 12 to 18 in. high – *Rhododendron sargentianum* with yellow flowers, *R. pemakoense,* lilac pink, *R. keleticum,* purple-crimson, and two blue-flowered *R. fastigiatum* which have in addition grey leaves. As a contrast I included a *Berberis gracilis nana* which for two years sat like a vegetable owl, but now has taken a fresh interest producing each April a most creditable crop of yellow flowers. Another berberis, *verruculosa,* is 30 in. high, a dome of hard green leaves which are silvered beneath. Wandering amongst them all is a yellow-flowered *Clematis tangutica* which is better used as ground cover than grown in the traditional way over a trellis. *Cornus canadensis* is not I suppose in the strict sense of the word a shrub as it dies back to soil level each year. I planted this along the beech hedge which borders one side of the plot, and now from a carpet of leaves it is starred with white flowers from late spring through to mid-summer. I also get the clustered heads of scarlet fruits.

Finally, in the coolest corner of the acid soil, I planted a *Mitchella repens.* This has proved almost too invasive, the procumbent stems rooting as they grow. However, the flowers and foliage are so quietly charming that I permit it rather more freedom than would be allowed to a lesser personality.

The composition of this piece of garden taxed my ingenuity to the utmost but gave me infinite pleasure also. Now, as it matures, I look for other ways to improve it, for such is the essence of gardening, changeless yet ever changing.

Tree Silhouettes

From November until March the garden and its surroundings rely on what could properly be termed silhouettes to provide beauty or interest. Indeed, in most cases, deciduous trees gain rather than lose their character as the leaves are shed. My memories of winter are richer and more clear cut than those of summer. With the inevitable clutter of vegetation at that time of the year the pictures tend to be amorphous no matter how lovely. The impact is general, rather than particular. I have Christmas memories of beech trees lined against the angry sunset of a snow-filled sky and of the dark outline of a farm in the Yorkshire Dales seen through birch, delicate as a Chinese woodcut in contrast to the man-made masonry. I remember, too, on a journey to Wales, a solitary Scots Pine at the head of a torrent-filled glen, green and gold and magnificent which left me wondering why with so much beauty around me, I bother to garden. Of all these remembered scenes the best loved is of silver birch, mixed with holly, Scots Pine, and rowan above a carpet of russet bracken relieved in part by the emerald green of the sphagnum moss. Surely man's love of even a small piece of wilderness must always remain.

In the garden, shrubs with a characteristic outline always play an important part although I may permit forsythia, mock orange, and other similar shapeless but magnificent shrubs to riot into a tangle, for their only beauty is in flower.

Few trees in winter can equal the beauty of our own native white-stemmed birch. I work every day surrounded by them, discovering fresh beauty in the delicate twig tracery, the elegant weeping habit, and the winter sunlight on the pale stems. Though *Prunus serrula* lacks the grace of the birch, the red-brown trunk like well-polished mahogany, has lightened the dank greyness of a hundred winter days. I grow it in a corner of the garden reserved for plants of strong personality, which has as its centrepiece a matriarchal, sombre yew. There also is a *Salix matsudana tortuosa,* whose twisted branches, the colour of meadow hay, are a delight with the wind-blown blue and white of a March sky behind. *Parrotia persica* is the vegetable counterpart of 'Fingal The Fair One', the squat rugged strength of the branches reproduces the character of the legendary hero. Always grow parrotia free, uncluttered with vegetation, yet balancing its strength with the tiered silver-grey beauty of the evergreen *Juniperus* x *media pfitzeriana.*

Trees must have played a part in my early life, for they figure largely in some of my happier memories of childhood. Spring can either be the

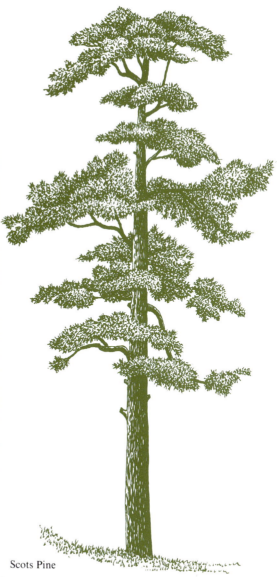

Scots Pine

Acer palmatum dissectum atropurpureum has such outstandingly beautiful foliage, only the arching grace of a fern provides a suitably elegant compliment.

The Corkscrew Willow, *Salix matsudana tortuosa*, is loveliest in spring as the young leaves break from the straw-coloured branches. Another shrub which will interest the dedicated flower arranger.

OPPOSITE: The contrasting shapes of the deciduous Weeping Birch, *Betula pendula youngii*, and a selection of conifers.

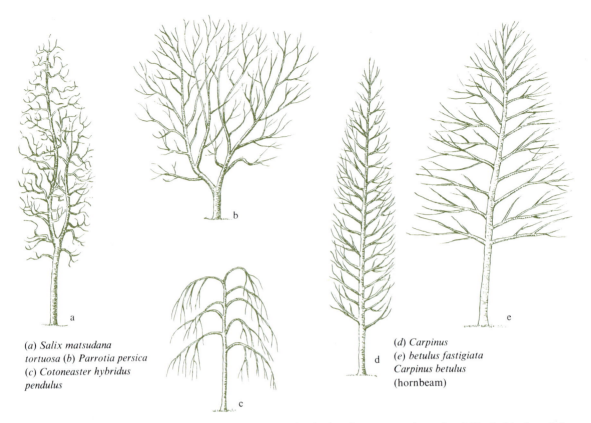

(a) *Salix matsudana tortuosa* (b) *Parrotia persica* (c) *Cotoneaster hybridus pendulus*

(d) *Carpinus* (e) *betulus fastigiata Carpinus betulus* (hornbeam)

cathedral splendour of grey beech stems rising from a carpet of thousands of snowdrops, or larch, soft in spring green, with primroses underneath.

Not all gardens can support the bulk of forest trees, yet it is still feasible to achieve a very satisfactory winter landscape in miniature. Various forms of Japanese Maple, *Acer palmatum,* even grown in pots will soon develop the mushroom-like, slightly windswept outline which makes them excellent plants for the heather or rock garden. For contrast I use a columnar conifer, erect, puritanically uncompromising as its bisects the horizontal lines. My favourite maple for this purpose is *dissectum atropurpureum,* which in addition to having an attractive rounded habit colours handsomely in the autumn.

That *Stranvaesia davidiana* is so frequently described as an erect branching shrub surprises me. I know three 20-year-old bushes at Harlow Car and all have developed an umbrella habit which I find becoming. Planted round with the evergreen hummocks of *Genista hispanica* it makes a perfect group to soften the hard angle between border and lawn. I see *Sorbus decora nana* (*S. scopulina*) every day in the summer, a

shaft of green against the hills behind and in winter the branches exhibit the same fastigiate habit. This rowan is good value for the small garden as it rarely exceeds 15 ft. in height.

Trees of pendulous outline are available in bewildering diversity, from the beech or weeping willow to the miniature charms of a standard-grown *Cotoneaster hybridus pendulus,* so it is relatively easy to suit most soils and situations. The birch, naturally pendulous, includes two elegant weeping varieties in *Betula pendula youngii,* a dome-shaped small tree, and the primly graceful *B. pendula tristis* which develops a neat symmetrical head, needing only a small area in which to grow.

In the winter hornbeam recovers individuality after spending the summer looking like a poor relation of the beech. Once the leaves go, all the masculine beauty of fluted stems and downward arching branches stands revealed. Strange that a tree such as this should give rise to *Carpinus betulus fastigiata* which makes a symmetrical pyramid, ideal for the small garden. Indeed, I use it to hide telegraph poles and similar ugly objects.

I try to consider my garden as a unit composed of plants, animals, birds and insects, so that some shrubs in addition to providing colour also supply food for the birds in the form of berries. One of the most graceful of all small pendulous shrubs is the evergreen *Cotoneaster salicifolius flocossus*. The narrow leaves are dark shining green on large drooping stems and in autumn it is bright with a mass of deep red berries. By Christmas the berries have all gone, and only the shrub's elegance remains to delight the gardener.

Sixteen years ago I planted a few specimens of *Erica arborea alpina* to add height to a rather flat corner of the heather garden. Now the plants are 4 ft. high and the soft green foliage on erect stems is seen in contrast to the bare branches of the birch woodland beyond adding a touch of welcome green to the inhospitable winter scene.

Conifers make all the difference to a winter landscape. There are varieties of all sizes from those suitable for growing in a window-box to the largest suitable for property many acres in extent. Remember, however, that it is easy to over plant and render the landscape formless. I shall mention only two groupings as examples of what for me is meant by garden silhouettes. The first grouping like so many other garden features started with one shrub, a specimen of *Chamaecyparis pisifera plumosa*, conical in outline and with feathery green foliage. Gradually over the years the picture was filled in first by adding *Chamaecyparis lawsoniana wisselii* which forms a narrow dark green column and then by planting, just to one side, a maple with its intricate twig pattern. Conifers play a dominant role in the second group which began with a specimen of *Juniperus* x *media pfitzeriana* and then had a *Chamaecyparis pisifera plumosa aurea* added for contrast with its yellow cone outline showing up well against the tiered grey-green of the juniper. Because this setting lacked a certain buoyancy I planted a silver birch behind and now find a great deal of pleasure from what is in effect a simple composition.

Silhouette gardening must be kept simple or it degenerates into an intolerable clutter. A group of bamboos with a single conifer or maple for company will say more than 10 acres of mixed woodland.

My regard for the cedars as specimen trees increases rather than decreases with the passing years. I have a picture of the magnificent Cedar of Lebanon with wrought iron gates in the foreground in the garden at Hidcote Manor,

Cedar of Lebanon

Gloucestershire which whenever I grow weary of endless rose pruning or hand weeding between marigolds, restores my faith in the virtue of trees as the ultimate of gardening achievement. Even against the storm wrack of an October sky this tree expressed serenity. In a small garden it is impossible, but there is a dwarf form possessed from any early age with all the parent's sturdy character, *Cedrus libani sargentii*. The short powerful stem and weeping habit make this a useful small garden tree. Mine is only 3 ft. high but planted high up in the rock garden, so that the sunshine brings out the full beauty of the blue-green foliage, it presents a wholly satisfying illusion of grandeur.

Another conifer which was bought after a visit to Windsor Park is *Chamaecyparis lawsoniana knowefieldensis*. I first saw this on a day of shower and sunshine and my immediate impression was that of a green waterfall cascading down the heather bank. Now I have a plant of my own tumbling down a slope in the rock garden and the deep green overlapping sprays of foliage look exactly like the ripples of a fast flowing stream. Though slow growing I take pleasure in watching my own plant grow into a most impressive silhouette.

Rhododendrons add a certain dignity to the landscape. *Rhododendron falconeri* towering 20 ft. above a highland glen is a sight to rejoice

Muscari are used as ground cover to the beautiful *Magnolia* x *soulangiana* in this delightful planting to welcome the spring.

Cotinus coggygria lights a beacon to herald the autumn as the green leaves turn to red and gold.

*Rhododendron
williamsianum*

the heart. Unfortunately, it does need shelter or the large leaves are damaged, and also space or everything around it is smothered. There are, however, smaller members of the genus which in flower are superb, but afterwards have a beauty of form or leaf which suit them admirably for inclusion in a chapter of this sort.

I grow *R. williamsianum* over an old oak stump in an attempt to emulate the superb specimen at Englingham, Northumberland, where it makes a perfect mound of rounded, heart-shaped leaves 30 in. high in bold relief against the white of a waterfall. In May the pink bell-shaped flowers are followed by the copper bronze of young growths.

Much of the joy I find in gardening is linked to brief moments of a beauty so all pervading that the recollection of it is sufficient to lift the dreariest days of bitter winter. Another picture, which is still fresh in my memory, is of *Rhododendron* Sir Charles Lemon. The foliage of this hybrid is blue-grey above, copper red beneath, and I first saw it against white birch stems patterned with February sunshine. The specimens here are 5 ft. in height by as much across.

I would hesitate to suggest planting bamboos in a small garden were it not for the fact that one of the finest specimens I know grows in a small garden where the soil is so well drained even the worms carry water bottles. The species in this case, and my own favourite, is *Arundinaria nitida*. The long gracefully arched branches are the epitomy of elegance and the canes which are flushed purple are furnished with long thin foliage. Associated with the bamboo is a beautifully grown specimen of *Prunus* Amanogawa, a small columnar tree, which in spring is transformed into a pillar of fragrant semi-double pink flowers. A more perfect contrast in shapes would be difficult to achieve.

I had grown the Corkscrew Hazel, *Corylus avellana contorta*, fourteen years just as a curiosity until one evening while tying in a rambling rose I saw the distorted branches with their pendant catkins against the orange-red of a March sunset. Now I cherish not one, but three plants, so that the opportunities of repeating the experience are trebled.

Conifers

I would consider a garden without evergreens, especially conifers, to be incomplete. Throughout the year they play an important role in providing a subtle contrast in shape and foliage texture and they are very valuable when the cold fingers of frost have stripped the foliage from deciduous trees.

There are species and varieties so slow growing that they will grow contentedly for a generation in the modest dimensions of a trough garden. At the other extreme the family includes trees that soar, 100 to 120 ft., majestic in their perfect symmetrical outline. No matter the size of garden – be the landscape formal or designed to harmonise with the natural scenery around – there are conifers of the right shape and foliage colour to fit and enhance the picture.

They adapt themselves to any but the most inhospitable soils, and there are few gardens incapable of supporting a selection of these fascinating plants.

Abies

The silver firs are so varied in character and soil requirements that were they not so fascinatingly beautiful I would exclude them all. The greater proportion have a characteristic outline which adds distinction to the landscape especially in winter. *Abies concolor,* the White Fir, is a magnificent specimen tree with grey bole and silver young shoots. It is rather large for any except the estate garden but there is a form to be recommended for the smaller garden known as *glauca compacta* which is so slow growing it may even be utilised in the rock garden.

Since seeing the specimen of *A. koreana* at Barnhourei, Kirkcudbrightshire, this is certainly my favourite of the genus. The leaves are dark green above, silver beneath which is particularly attractive when seen against the violet-blue cones which are produced even on very small specimens. The habit is neat, conical in outline, and certainly it will take many years to outgrow even a garden of the most modest size.

Seed offers a means of increase which I avail myself of whenever fresh stock is required.

Chamaecyparis lawsoniana wisselii

Whenever I see *Abies koreana*, I remember the quiet garden, full of bird song and the sound of rushing water, where I first saw this superb conifer.

Chamaecyparis obtusa crippsii is an elegant slow-growing conifer which gives an impression of lightness not usually exhibited by the denser-habited varieties. The fern-like sprays of golden foliage look particularly lovely when contrasted with a ground planting of heathers.

Junipers are discovered in such a variety of shapes there is surely one to fit most situations. The narrowly erect habit of the Irish Juniper rarely exceeds 10 to 12ft in height.

A conifer which takes on autumn colour without shedding its leaves is *Pinus sylvestris aurea*. This form of our native Scots Pine turns yellow for the autumn and reverts to normal green in spring.

Juniperus x *media pfitzeriana*

Cedrus

The Mount Atlas Cedar, *Cedrus atlantica*, in this garden has reached 11 ft. in 9 years, a green inspiring cone of a plant. *C. atlantica glauca*, the Blue Cedar, is slower growing, but the silvered leaves are very fine even on a small tree. *C. deodara* has branches which droop at the tips in a most effective way and the glaucous leaves are in contrast to the delicate green breaking buds in spring. *C. libani*, the Cedar of Lebanon, is slow but in maturity a majestic sight, dark green but never sombre. Two dwarf forms *nana* and *sargentii* grace the small rock outcrop in my garden.

Chamaecyparis

Chamaecyparis lawsoniana, Lawson's Cypress, makes a tall tree and is useful as a windbreak or screen to hide some ugly part of the view beyond the garden. I would use a selected form like Green Hedger for often seedlings show a wide variation in ultimate height. Selected forms include *allumii* which is often used in tubs or on terraced walks for the growth is upright and the colour glaucous blue, and *ellwoodii* which is very slow growing, with feathery graceful leaves and an ultimate height of between 8 and 10 ft. *Erecta* makes a pyramid of light green while the grey feathery-leaved *fletcheri* has a tendency to

spread under heavy weights of snow, but it is still a worthy contender for a place in the garden. *Wisselii* is the most tightly erect of all and in youth its branching pattern shows a whirled effect. I nip the top out of the cuttings to encourage this. *C. obtusa nana* is a jewel with tight fans of mossy green leaves and a neat and compact habit. *C. obtusa crippsii* is a small slow-growing loosely conical tree and it makes one of the loveliest small garden conifers.

The various forms of Sawara Cypress, *Chamaecyparis pisifera*, fit easily into the landscape without the somewhat alien aspect sometimes presented by the hybrids of *lawsoniana*. *C. pisifera* and its varieties make delicately poised light foliage trees. *C. pisifera plumosa* and the *aurea* form are especially pleasing planted as a group with the greyish-green leafage of the former contrasting well against the soft feathery gold of the *aurea*.

Cupressus

Cupressus macrocarpa rivals *Cupressocyparis leylandii* (see hedging plants) for speed, and is a valuable hedging and shelter belt tree on the coast. I have plants in my garden which are 12 years old and each winter I expect the worst, but providing they are left unclipped all seems to be well. The golden form *lutea* is a delightful shrub with soft yellow foliage.

Ginkgo

I only know *Ginkgo biloba,* the Maidenhair Tree, from the specimen growing in my garden, though I have seen some fine well-grown trees elsewhere. No one can truly understand a plant until they have lived with it, but one thing it does need is a well-drained soil or it mopes in a most unmaidenly manner. The fan-shaped leaves from which it gets its name turn a pleasing shade of yellow in autumn.

Juniperus

Contented on acid or alkaline soils, I use the genus extensively especially in the ground-hugging forms. They are so useful for covering steep banks or manhole covers, bad workmanship in rock gardens or marking the edge of a drive.

Juniperus communis is our own native juniper and as such should be duly honoured. It is indestructibly hardy and has served me well in a dozen unpromising places. Though found in the wild growing mainly on lime soils, it has accepted acid, ill-drained clay with no outward signs of bad health. The various forms of the species show the same adaptability. *Compressa,* a cone-shaped midget, makes an ideal plant for a trough or small rock garden, taking about 18 years to reach a height of 12 in. A wide-spreading, ground-hugging bush, *depressa* is excellent for clothing steep slopes in the rock garden. *Prostrata* is of a similar habit.

The Creeping Juniper, *Juniperus horizontalis,* is a remarkable conifer. A single specimen in 10 years will cover an area of 18 sq. ft. The leaves are a lovely glaucous grey in summer and silver purple in winter. *Douglasii* and Bar Harbor, a shade taller growing, both have the blue-grey colour which becomes a rich plum purple with the onset of winter. There are few better ways of clothing a steep slope with easy to maintain attractive foliage than by a selection of prostrate dwarf conifers, including always at least one form of *J. horizontalis.*

Juniperus x *media* is one of the classifications conveniently devised by botanists as a lumber room in which to push everything which will not fit elsewhere. Undoubtedly, *J.* x *media pfitzeriana* is an integral part of any conifer planting I ever plan. It is a wide spreading tiered shrub with the branchlets showing a becoming tendency to droop at the tips. Quietly dressed in attractive grey-green, it is a comfortably handsome shrub in every respect. *J.* x *media pfitzeriana aurea* is a valuable addition to my collection, the young growth breaks soft yellow in the summer, changing to bronze in the winter.

The list could be extended ad infinitum, but I shall restrict the section on junipers to just two more species. *J. sabina,* the Savin Juniper, and *J. squamata* have a fragrance which some object to, but I quite enjoy. A form of *J. sabina tamariscifolia* has a determinedly prostrate form of growth and makes a good rich green ground cover. *J. squamata meyeri,* on the other hand, can show variation, some grow rather loosely while others are fastigiate. I prefer the plant in my garden which grows up, then the branches arch over at the tips.

Libocedrus

Libocedrus decurrens columnaris is a tree so upright that it almost expresses a parsimonious austerity in a determination not to exceed by a yard the space allocated. I plant it in groups of three against a foreground of shrubs with horizontally tiered branching arrangements such as *Viburnum tomentosum* Lanarth. Grown in this way the dark green outline is seen to full advantage. Single specimens add distinction to the characterless glass-box architecture which is spreading like a festering disease over the British Isles.

Picea

This genus includes the Norway Spruce, *Picea abies,* which is so welcome in every home at Christmas time. When planted in a sheltered place it will make a shapely tree of pyramidal outline. There are several dwarf forms without which no rock garden landscape is really complete.

Picea abies clanbrassiliana is a dense, slow-growing shrub rather like a prickly puff ball. *Picea abies nidiformis* is really like a bird's nest in shape, a perfectly circular flat-topped shrub, pale green in spring, darker in summer. I had a magnificent specimen in the corner of the rock garden which was unfortunately killed by passing dogs.

Picea breweriana is the loveliest of all conifers. The pendulous side branches several feet long

Clematis Hagley Hybrid and American Pillar rose making a riot of colour which would look lovely planted against a grey stone wall.

Clematis which have many petalled flowers need to be trained out so each stem has a fair share of space. The flowers like those displayed by Countess of Lovelace can then be enjoyed individually.

The long pendant catkins of the male form of *Garrya elliptica*, to the undisguised delight of flower arrangers, are produced during the winter months when other material is in short supply.

Picea breweriana

change colour with each passing breeze, like a silken green curtain, first dark then light green. It is rather tall for the smaller garden for after about fifty years it will reach 40 ft.

Pinus

The pines always hint of vast mountain landscapes, the wide sweep of the Yorkshire Moors, the quiet of a tree-lined loch. I like them about the place because of their beauty and the

atmosphere they bring. Like all creatures of wind-scourged places they fret and die in a smoke-polluted atmosphere. They are quite happy in a wide range of soils, and will make shift to survive in material only a ling would compete for.

Pinus cembra makes a reasonable-sized tree which in maturity has a lot of charm. The variety *chlorocarpa* is a wide-spreading bush with silvered leaves which earns covetous glances wherever it is planted. *P. mugo pumilio* is just about the ultimate vegetable product. It makes a low spreading bush with tufts of needles stuck out in the most remarkable way. I find it irresistably ugly and wonder how it survives my sometimes pungent comments.

The native Scots Pine, *P. sylvestris,* is one of the loveliest of conifers, the orange-red bark of the bole is in sharp contrast to the dark green foliage. *Pumila* is the dwarf form, making a rounded glaucous-leaved bush which is more suitable than its towering parent for the small garden.

Taxus

People fortunate enough to inherit a garden which includes mature specimens of this genus should be thankful at being so singularly blessed, for the yew is an ornamental evergreen of great worth. In the woodland near my home they seed themselves under oak and birch, seeming to like the shade which few trees do. In the open they make a dark background for the gaily flowered deciduous shrubs. As a hedge its value has already been noted in the chapter on hedges.

Taxus baccata is a native plant surrounded by a wealth of legend. Like many other trees long cultivated in gardens it has given rise to several variants. *Adpressa* makes a dense shrub which tends to form several leaders but I prefer the golden-leaved *aurea* for the way its leaves cheer up a dull February day.

The Irish Yew, *T. b. fastigiata,* is an erect-growing variety, tailor made for lining a formal walk. *Fastigiata aurea,* the golden form is even slower growing but equally attractive. *Horizontalis* is a good ground cover in heavy shade, showing no ambition to grow up, always out. I grow two plants, one under *Acer campestre,* the other hangs down masking a large stone in the stream garden. *T. media hicksii* is rather more angular in branch arrangement than the type,

Pinus mugo pumilio

*Taxus baccata
fastigiata*

less dense with lighter green foliage. It makes an elegant specimen of unusual appearance.

Thuja

Thuja expresses once again the versatility of many conifers. It provides species suitable for hedging, windbreaks, specimen trees, and dwarf-growing forms for the small garden. *Thuja occidentalis ellwangeriana aurea* is a soft-yellow-leaved form, good in summer and in winter for lighting the dullness of the borders. A deeper yellow form, Rheingold, has foliage which turns to golden bronze in October, a

slow-growing shrublet which takes many years to reach 6 ft.

Thuja orientalis elegantissima, a pyramidal form, is useful as an accent point amongst heathers, or at the junction of a path and rock outcrop.

A fast-growing ornamental tree, *T. plicata* has glossy green leaves and is pleasantly scented, especially noticeable after rain during spring and summer. It stands clipping well so makes a good informal hedge. *Hillieri,* a well-furnished, slow growing variety does on occasions throw up ugly naked shoots which should be carefully cut away with a sharp knife or secateurs. It does, however, lack a definite shape which makes the impact on the garden seem rather less than would be expected of a conifer.

Chamaecyparis, cupressocyparis, juniperus, and thuja all root readily from cuttings taken in September or in the case of cupressocyparis in February. I use a 1 peat, 2 sand mixture, and leave the cuttings in the frame until really well rooted before potting them up, or lining them out. Picea, though not quite so easy, will root a modest percentage in the same medium taken in September. Taxus are slow but will eventually develop roots from semi-mature terminal shoots which are 3 in. long and just firming at the base. Usually August or early September is a suitable period.

The large leaves of
*Hedera colchica dentata
variegata* are
attractively shaded
green, grey and cream.
The plant is perfectly
impervious to the
weather if given the
protection of a wall but
when grown in the
open the leaves can be
browned by the cold
east wind.

Hydrangea petiolaris is
a strong-growing
climber with the
commendable ability to
support itself by means
of aerial roots. I dislike
having to spend time
tying up wall plants
every year and so I
have a particular
affection for those
plants which do not
demand my help.

The almost
indestructible hardiness
of Winter Jasmine,
Jasminum nudiflorum,
and the cheerful colour
the yellow flowers bring
to the dark days of
winter make this shrub
a prime favourite.
Excellent when trained
over a wall or fence.

I have several species of
honeysuckle scattered
at strategic intervals
around the garden.
They are planted close
to frequently used paths
so that everyone who
passes can enjoy the
fragrance of this
cottage-garden flower.

Climbers and Wall Plants

stand the roots out from the wall, especially if there is an overhang, as this saves desperate endeavours with the watering-can rescuing drought-exhausted plants.

The owners of small gardens need to utilise every scrap of space and they, therefore, must be more selective in their choice of plants. Climbers and wall plants will provide the answer to many problems for they will add both space and height to congested sites and will bring colour to every available wall. However, enthusiasm should be tempered with discreet understanding for there are climbers which love to be baked into brilliance of flower by hot sun, whereas others must be soothed by moist shade. Some climbers, of which *Actinidia chinensis* and *Polygonum baldschuanicum* are prime examples, will swallow a house completely so quickly do they grow. Others like wisteria or clematis must be carefully pruned and trained, or the gardener is left to contemplate a naked expanse of stem. No matter what treasured climber is planted, the wall will provide a protection not enjoyed by the denizens of the open garden.

Before attempting any planting examine the soil at the foot of an average house wall. Usually it consists of builders' leavings, sub-soil, pot crocks and other aridities, possibly enriched by a few tea leaves. All this must be excavated and replaced with soil from a fertile part of the garden. A good mixture consists of 5 parts of garden soil to 2 parts of peat plus a 6-in. pot of bonemeal to every barrowload of the mixture. Only a narrow border need be made, 2 ft. wide by 15 in. deep, for given a good start healthy roots will penetrate less profitable fields.

Climbers need not be confined to walls. Stumps of old trees, venerable apple or other fruit trees, chain-link fencing, indeed anything capable of supporting the extra weight can be pressed into service as a foster home to a clematis or rambler rose. The soil improvement is just as necessary in each case. When planting

Clematis montana

Actinidia kolomikta

For climbers some support will be necessary and modern invention provides a richly varied choice. A well-made wooden trellis, plastic-covered mesh, vine eyes with wire stretched between, or a nail hammered in where required – there is something to suit every depth of pocket. I use trellis or plastic-covered netting fitted to wooden bobbins 2 in. long, made by cutting up a broom shaft. This holds the plants out from the wall so that the air can circulate freely reducing the incidence of mildew and red spider mite. If wood is used anywhere as a support it should be treated with a good preservative first.

Some climbers like ivy need no support other than that provided by their aerial roots whereas others, as for example the climbing roses, need tying in with string, plastic ribbon, webbing or a similar artificial aid. I always use a soft string which will not chafe even the most tender bark and, which is perhaps more important, it will rot after a year or two. When indestructible material is used I grow careless about the annual inspection to ensure the stem is not being constricted by the tie. All wall plants must be looked over at least twice a year to make certain the stems are not being chafed or strangled by the supporting media.

I could fill a book with a selection of climbing and wall plants but as before will restrict the choice to those which have been proven in the crucible of the garden.

Actinidia

There are two species especially suitable for wall culture but both need different treatment. *Actinidia chinensis* will riot over an acre of wall in an undignified scramble. The large leaves, 6 to 8 in. across, and fragrant flowers are recompense enough if space can be provided, but really only a castle offers sufficient wall space and even then, should the drawbridge be left down, it could prove a liability for once inside it would take over the uppermost turret. *A. kolomikta* is a shrub of feminine complexity. It is incapable of deciding on a suitable leaf colour, the lower half remaining green while the upper half turns white and pink. I avoid hard pruning for the stems being hollow tend to die back along the whole branch. A thinning of the twigs is a permitted indulgence. A warm south or west-facing wall suits actinidia best.

Ceanothus

Although ceanothus can be grown as a bush in the open garden, it is only happy in the colder gardens when given wall protection. However, it is worth all the devotion lavished on it. I remember a very old house in Hurworth, County Durham, which supported an enormous specimen of the variety A. T. Johnson. The brick mellowed by age to a warm buff pink made an

A lovely specimen of *Parthenocissus tricuspidata* covered the centuries-old vicarage in my home village in the Dales with a mantle of scarlet every October. It is a homely plant which will add character to a colourless wall.

Vitis coignetiae is a strong-growing vine with large rounded leaves which in autumn turn scarlet. A most spectacular covering for an ugly building or tree.

OPPOSITE: Few climbers excite the instant admiration that a well-grown wisteria in full bloom commands.

ideal background to the blue flowers. See main list for full description.

Chaenomeles

See main list.

Clematis

Glorious in flower, on occasions regally temperamental, this richly endowed genus must surely lay strong claim to contain the most beautiful climbers ever to grace our gardens. As I stand each spring under a 30-ft. high hawthorn through which has intertwined a *Clematis montana* Elizabeth I would be the last to disagree. The white of the hawthorn and pink of the clematis intermingle to make the complete floral curtain. Tradition has it that clematis produce their best efforts when the roots are shaded but the flowers are allowed to reach up into the sun. However, I believe a well-drained soil to be more important, otherwise losses in winter are liable to be heavy. A mulch of peat mixed with a handful of bonemeal is all the feed necessary.

I grow *C. alpina* through and amongst deciduous rhododendrons. It comes so readily from seed that some of my experimental plantings border on the reckless. Nothing, however, matches a plant I saw in the wild growing through *Rhododendron ferrugineum*. The blue flowers with a central boss of white stamens overlaid the brick-red blooms of the rhododendron like a Spanish mantilla.

Few things are harder to make an impression on than a well-seasoned oak stump. It took several heart-rending hours with an axe to convince me of this. Eventually I planted a *C. x jouiniana* in front of it and now the stump is hidden by a sprawling network of branches which from July to August are covered by white, lilac-tinted flowers. Cote d'Azur is a form of the above with leathery hard foliage and azure-blue flowers. Probably the violet-blue blooms of *C. x jackmanii* are the best known of all the genus, appearing as they do during the holiday months of July to September and this hybrid has given rise to many large-flowered garden varieties.

Some gardeners have an instinct for putting flowers in just the right association with one another and I am fortunate in that for 15 years just such an artist gave me endless help at Harlow Car. *C. macropetala,* an early-summer-flowering

Clematis macropetala

species with large violet semi-double blooms, was her favourite and it was always grown through a wisteria which flowered at the same time. *C. montana* is the robust, independent, 'go out and conquer the world' member of the clan, growing well in any position. I have seen it on walls, potting sheds, thatched cottages, Scots Pine, apple trees, even a ruined church. I grow the white form *grandiflora,* the rose-purple-flowered, bronze-leaved *rubens* and the pearl-pink, sweetly fragrant Elizabeth. All flower in May and some years a small second crop appears rather apologetically in August.

The species grow readily from seed or cuttings, and the most obliging of all is *C. tangutica.* Some years ago I tried three plants in a limestone rock garden and they are now very much at home rambling about amongst the stones. The flower stems are 12 in. long, each topped with a deep yellow, Chinese lantern-like flower. These are followed in due season by silver seed heads which in their own way equal the beauty of the blooms.

Internodal cuttings should be made in August–September and placed in pumice or peat and sand mixture.

Of the larger-flowered garden hybrids there must be a plant to suit every taste – large,

Clematis
Etoile Violette

pruning usually reserved for roses. Immediately the buds break in spring I cut the top back to within 6 to 10 in. of ground level. The young tender shoots which break after this cavalier treatment are protected from the depredations of slugs and when long enough tied in to canes so that they are not damaged by strong winds or a bad shot with the push hoe. The initial training during the first year is very simply to build up a good framework and stop the bad habit most varieties inherit of producing long weak shoots which can collapse overnight with clematis wilt. Pruning after this is regulated according to the group into which the varieties fall. For example, the Lanuginosa group which includes Lady Northcliffe, a hybrid with deep lavender flowers which I grow on a north wall, and Mrs Hope which intermingles with Winter Jasmine on a west wall, opening mauve flowers barred with a deeper blue continuously through August into September, are pruned in February each year. If the growth comes persistently from below the mulch as with Lady Northcliffe, cut the shoots back to an inch above soil level. Where there is a stem before the plant branches as with Mrs Hope, prune the previous season's growth back to within two buds of this. I use exactly the same treatment for the Viticella and Jackmanii groups.

I just let the *alpina* and *montana* hybrids grow where space permits, then cut them back to within two or three buds of the old wood in early March. Where space is limited I train them out to make a framework of branches to fill the available wall space. The first two years I tip these framework branches hard to make them thicken. After this the young growths which break from them are spur pruned in September to within two inches of the old wood. Specialists cut even closer, but I lack the courage. In fact, I rarely restrict either *alpina* or *montana* hybrids, preferring them growing free and untrammelled.

The Patens group, which includes my particular favourite Nelly Moser, are just thinned judiciously spacing out the remaining shoots to cover the available space. I do this in September, then all that is needed during March the next year is a little spring clean of dead wood. Some writers of text books recommend doing the work in February but their gardens must be a good deal warmer than mine for all I want to do in February is work in the greenhouse.

Possibly one of the reasons I like *C.* x *jouiniana*

medium or small flowers in pink, purple, blue or white. I only include a selection here for like legion they are many. First Barbara Jackman (Patens) which I grow on a north-west wall, the petunia-pink flowers are better in partial shade. Comtesse de Bouchaud (Jackmanii) is profligate with her pink flowers from July to October. Ernest Markham (Viticella) is rather spoilt for me as I first saw the dark red velvety flowers against new brick; the gardener was at fault not the clematis. In vigour and length of flowering season, July to October, it cannot be faulted. My affection for the gentle and beautiful Etoile Violette (Viticella), the first clematis which ever grew for me when I was 12 years old, has never diminished. It has deep violet blossoms and yellow stamens. For a white-painted north wall there is either Nelly Moser (Patens), pale mauve-pink with a carmine bar in June and again in autumn, or Perle d'Azur (Jackmanii), a special favourite and the longest-flowering pale blue with the faintest bar down each petal. I have only grown Hagley Hybrid (Jackmanii) for two years but it is fast becoming a favourite of mine. Its rosy-mauve flowers are borne freely. Countess of Lovelace (Florida) has bluish-violet, double rosette-shaped flowers in early summer.

I give newly planted clematis the ruthless

so much is that it needs no pruning. I even make an attempt to grow the evergreen *C. armandii* for the same reason. Unfortunately, in my exposed garden, I am vouchsafed a crop of the fragrant clusters of pure white flowers only one year in three.

Cotoneaster

Those which make good wall shrubs are detailed in the main list.

Eccremocarpus

Eccremocarpus scaber may not be absolutely hardy in every garden, but since it will grow enthusiastically from seed to flower in 6 months this need not be regarded too seriously. I take unpardonable liberties with the plant, growing

Eccremocarpus scaber

it up through shrubs in the borders and on a house wall, but the happiest idea of all that I have found is letting it mingle with ivy on a sycamore stump. The orange-scarlet flowers and compound leaves look even brighter against the hard green of the ivy.

Forsythia

I used to be rather intolerant of *Forsythia suspensa* until one day, when travelling to

Lancaster, I noticed a shrub which had turned an old grey stone wall lemon with a riot of flowers. This, I was assured, was *F. suspensa fortunei* carefully trained out on the wall for something like 150 sq. ft. A west or south wall would enable the wood to ripen fully.

Garrya

Garrya elliptica is without doubt the most maligned shrub in my garden. With serene good nature it presents a well-clothed aspect of grey-green to hide the nakedness of a very exposed west wall. In February come the silver catkins 5 in. long to delight everyone who sees it, except me. Despite every effort on my part the garrya and I have not yet reached a rapprochement. Cuttings taken of young wood in July–August root readily. One I took 16 years ago is now 8 ft. high by about 6 ft. across.

Hedera helix sagittaefolia

Hedera

There is an old elm nearby clothed in ivy which confirms my regard for this climber. It makes a perfect sanctuary for nesting birds in summer, a column of polished green to lighten the dark days of winter. Some older buildings would be stark ruins without a softening mantle of ivy. No matter that the soil is dry to the point of aridity, or dark with the shade of forest trees, the ivy grows to mask the nakedness of inhospitable earth with quiet efficiency.

The common species, *Hedera helix,* has no equal as a self-clinging climber or for all-round adaptability. Fortunately, it shows no reluctance to sport new varieties to such an extent that the choice is becoming bewildering in its diversity. Buttercup, as the name implies, is a good yellow form, which dare I whisper it, always has the same effect on me as flat lemonade. *Congesta* is slow growing with small grey-green leaves. It is a fine plant for a terraced corner or a large stone in the rock garden. *Discolor* has leaves which change colour I discovered last year, dark green most of the year but in May–June cream and pink tinted. I cherish *marginata* on the east wall of my house, beautiful triangular leaves edged with cream, and in winter flushed with red. The Arrow Head Ivy, *H. h. sagittaefolia*, went into the garden because it outgrew the greenhouse and will I hope transform a Doric column from dark masonry to warm green.

There are also several good varieties of *H. colchica*, Persian Ivy, including *dentata variegata* with leaves shaded green, grey and cream; and Paddy's Pride with leaves in various tones of yellow and green. Both varieties would do well in a patio garden.

Propagation is by self-layering shoots or cuttings in July. I do the clipping in May when the growth is rapid enough to hide the scars.

Hydrangea

Hydrangea petiolaris is often recommended for a north wall, and while it will admittedly tolerate shade it responds with such alacrity to a position in full sun that I rather pander to it in this respect. The white flowers open in July above the heart-shaped leaves which themselves turn at the first touch of autumn frost to soft yellow. A clematis or the eccremocarpus will add a colourful overtone to the self-clinging hydrangea. Cuttings or layers offer the best results if further plants are required.

Jasminum

No climber does more to lift the grey pall of February than *Jasminum nudiflorum*. The yellow flowers on a north or west wall brave snow or arctic frost with equanimity. Over a low wall, on a trellis, clipped as an ornament to the front lawn, few soils or situations reduce Winter Jasmine to despair. Each flowering shoot should be cut back in April to within 2 shoots of the base.

The White Jasmine, *J. officinale*, is more circumspect, preferring to flower in the somnolence of July, lingering on until September. The sweetly scented white flowers festooned the tool shed at home where the roots were buried in mortar rubble, but refuse utterly to survive on wet clay, to my eternal regret. Cuttings taken with a heel in August will root readily enough.

Kerria

If a certain Dales cottage is any indication, *Kerria japonica* makes a good wall plant but needs careful pruning to avoid untidiness. Well-grown plants will fill a dark corner with rich yellow flowers. See main list.

Lonicera

The honeysuckle may be the foresters' curse, but to thousands it conjures up memories of twilight evenings rich with all the fragrance of red and gold woodbine. Over a pergola, clustering the rampart of a bridge, or through the boughs of an apple tree this common hedgerow plant is a delight in July and August. A position in full shade suits it best simulating as it does its natural woodland habitat.

Lonicera x *americana* is a vigorous climber which will spread 30 ft. The flowers appear earlier than those of the native woodbine in June to July, white at first, then yellow tinged with plum purple. *L. henryi* is another climber which needs room to spread and is almost worth the space for the beauty of the dark evergreen leaves. The red and yellow flowers are rather small and the blue-black berries soon disappear down some bird gourmet's rapacious throat.

Lonicera japonica is tender, or possibly intolerant of the heavy clay here, but flourishes in better-favoured gardens. It is partially evergreen and when grown in a cold greenhouse the pale, rather inconspicuous flowers are possessed of a delicate, attractive fragrance. It should be given a sheltered corner possibly on a summer house wall so that all the redolence of the flowers can be enjoyed.

The form of *L. japonica* known as *aureoreticulata* has proved more resilient in my garden than the type plant and softens, with golden-yellow variegated leaves, the hard out-

Lonicera japonica aureo-reticulata

Parthenocissus henryana

line of a millstone grit boulder in the rock garden. *L. periclymenum* is the woodbine and its variety *belgica* makes the perfect company planting. The first crop of yellow-flushed dark red flowers opens early in June to be followed in September by a late indulgence of the same quality if not the quantity. Softwood cuttings in July root rapidly in the sand frame. To prune shorten back the side shoots to 4 buds after flowering in September.

Parthenocissus

The Virginia creepers are especially noteworthy for brilliance of autumn colouring. *Parthenocissus henryana* is a Chinese climber which I use to disguise a rather unimaginative iron fence. Now the rusty iron has disappeared under a panoply of leaves which are tinged purple in the shade, but all turn deep red in autumn. *P. quinquefolia* from North America is the true Virginia creeper, a self-clinging species whose leaves turn scarlet and gold with the first frost of autumn; a vigorous plant which will cover a three storey building, chimney included. I remember a vicarage, centre of a lovely Yorkshire Dales' village which in October each year became a picture when covered by the scarlet leaves of *P. tricuspidata*. In good soil or poor sand the only variable feature is the size of the leaves.

Trimming is usually carried out in early May, clearing windows, gutters, and chimneys.

Polygonum

Polygonum baldschuanicum is a heaven-sent climber for those unfortunate gardeners with ugly buildings to cover, chain-link fences to hide, or air-raid shelters to disguise. My particular *bête noir* is a tarred shed. In three years the Russian Vine has covered it completely, even growing through the cracks amongst the tools hanging on the walls inside. White flowers tinted pink open throughout the late summer into autumn. Grown up an oak or similar sturdy support it becomes a curtain of white flower and pale green leaf. Cuttings of the short side branches taken during July – August root without difficulty.

Pyracantha

Pyracanthas make good wall shrubs. Clipped to

Polygonum baldschuanicum

a green buttress they take the square angularity from the modern concrete buildings which hold no pretence to architectural elegance. For a full description see main list.

Rosa

Some varieties of roses tried in gardens all over the British Isles gain, but above all hold a place in popular esteem, and it is these worthy perennials I consider first when presented with a new trellis or wall to cover.

Albéric Barbier is a cottage garden rambler rose with blooms that open yellow and turn white with age, and they are quince scented. Albertine is another rambler with glossy, dark green leaves, and two-toned flowers of copper and pink which are sweetly fragrant. American Pillar, once an extremely popular rambler, has deep pink flowers carried in clustered heads.

Caroline Testout has been a firm favourite for many years with large individual flowers of clear pink and good substance. Casino is a comparatively modern introduction with soft yellow flowers but it is not quite so vigorous as I would like.

Etude is one of the most satisfactory climbers to come into my garden in recent years. It is perpetually in bloom with flat-topped blossoms which are a beautiful silver pink and last well in winter when cut. Golden Showers on a pillar or rustic trellis makes a brilliant show over several weeks.

Maigold is a splendidly exuberant yellow rose, splashed with scarlet. The dark green glossy foliage and vigour make this an altogether companiable climber.

New Dawn will cover outbuilding, walls, trellis, tree stump or fence at a quite remarkable rate. Indeed, its robustness can be a hazard in a small garden. Fortunately, it is repeat flowering with blooms of a good rain-resistant pink.

I would never plant Zéphirine Drouhin in a sheltered place as it gets mildew badly unless the wind can blow through and around it. As a hedge supported on a trellis it is supreme and perpetually in flower from June until November. The flowers are carmine pink in colour, and scented as all roses should be.

Perpetual-flowering climbers are very much the mode and in addition to those already mentioned Danse du Feu, orange-red; Hamburger Phoenix, crimson and disease resistant, and Pink Perpetue are varieties well worthy of consideration.

Schizophragma

Schizophragma hydrangeoides is thought by many gardeners to be superior to the climbing hydrangea which it resembles. In my experience it is not so tolerant of poor soils as the hydrangea. In spite of this small failing it is a first-class, self-clinging climber. The flowers are certainly better. They are large and pale yellow, and are accompanied by leaves which turn deep gold in the autumn. Grown with the climbing rose Etude, whose silver-pink flowers open right through the summer, it transforms a wall from mediocrity to beauty in a few short years.

Vitis

The ornamental vines have for a long time been favourites of mine. Their leaves turn the most thought-provoking colours in the autumn from rose to deep wine purple. All leaves have a characteristic fragrance; those of the vine are positively alcoholic.

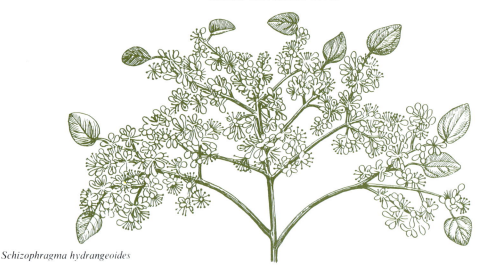

Schizophragma hydrangeoides

All need deep fertile soil to develop the largest possible leaves. The tendril climbing species are suitable for retaining walls, pergolas or terraces whereas the self-clinging species will cover a sun-warmed wall very quickly. I keep the roots fenced in, for a vine runs riot unless restricted. *Vitis coignetiae* is the one I know better than any other having grown it for twenty odd years. The leaves are large, 10 in. across in some I measured, and they turn to orange and dull crimson in late September. That beautiful plant *V. inconstans* must now because of a botanical whim be *Parthenocissus tricuspidata veitchii. Vitis pulchra* colours a warm red with the onset of winter and it is not unlike *V. coignetiae.*

The various forms of the Common Grape Vine, *V. vinifera*, are grown for ornament rather than fruit. Only the most optimistic would expect a profitable return from a vine outdoors except in a few favoured localites. The form known as *apiifolia* or Parsley Vine is enjoying a burst of popularity not previously recorded because of a growing interest in flower arranging. The deeply divided leaves are interesting, but would merit more attention if they changed colour in autumn instead of remaining morosely green. *Purpurea,* the Dyers Grape, is a plant for a white-washed wall to contrast with the deep purple colouring of the leaves. On the whole I enjoy the colour when they first open a deep red.

Layering in April into a peat and sand compost is the easiest method of propagation.

Wisteria

Even out of flower I find the gnarled, tortured

Wisteria

branches of the wisteria attractive. In full blossom there can be few more beautiful climbing shrubs. One of the loveliest associations I have ever seen was when wisteria was used to cover an old arch over a clear pool and cascade. The warm stone, exquisite flowers, and soothing music of running water captured a peace denied to most gardens. Where the twining shoots are allowed complete freedom, as when growing over a tall tree, little pruning is possible. Those growing in a restricted area, like a house wall, will need restraint to produce a proper crop of blossoms. I usually cut back the long shoots yielded annually to about 2 or 3 buds in August. Once a framework is established, spur pruning can be done in November, cutting to within 3 in. of the old wood. A shrub of such quality should be given the choice position on a sun-baked wall so the wood will ripen thoroughly. The species most often planted, *Wisteria chinensis* (*sinensis*) has fragrant flowers which are deep mauve in colour and carried in long racemes. There is a variety with double flowers called *W. floribunda* or the Japanese Wisteria which is variable in the matter of raceme length, and to be certain of a good display it is advisable to choose either the variety *alba* with white flowers, or *macrobotrys,* a beautiful variety with lilac flowers feathered purple in enormous pendant clusters, 24 in. long.

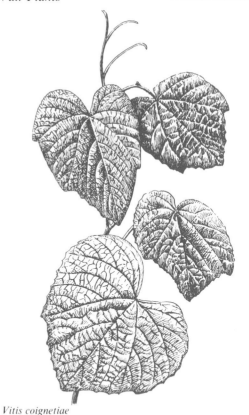

Vitis coignetiae

Planted with a laburnum on a pergola so that the flowers hang through, it makes a sight to uplift the most flagging spirit.

Part 2

An A-Z of Shrubs & Small Trees

A GLANCE at any reputable nurseryman's catalogue will give an indication of just how easy, and expensive, it can be to stock a large garden with a representative collection of shrubs. Indeed the owner of a bare plot of earth can become a thing obsessed, his life governed by the sole pursuit of plants to hide the nakedness. In this case the proverb 'act in haste, repent at leisure' becomes ever more true with each passing year as shrubs grow into a riotous tangle, trees grow up to overshadow the house, so that eventually only an axe and saw will restore some semblance of order. Whatever flights of fancy the gaily coloured illustrations in the catalogue may encourage, the hard school of experience has taught me to make all the main plantings of shrubs which have proved absolutely above suspicion in reliability and hardiness. I do not care if every other garden in the kingdom rejoices in groves of forsythia, ribes, syringa, and potentilla. This only makes me more determined to use them whenever possible, for what better recommendation can there be than this, that these, so-called common shrubs, will give of their best under all sorts of improbable combinations of soil and climate.

Acer

The fact that the redoubtable sycamore is a member of this noble clan may prove a cause for reflection amongst the more sober-minded gardeners. However, contained in this genus are some of the loveliest moderate-sized trees for foliage it is possible to cultivate.

Acer circinatum, the Vine Maple, was at first try a most reluctant debutante at Harlow Car, largely because I succeeded each time in planting it near a subterranean sulphur spring. Finally on the third move I selected a dry site and it is now a flourishing large shrub. The leaves are lovely in summer when they are shaded with bronze tones and in autumn they turn deep yellow and crimson.

Acer davidii makes a medium-sized tree of 30 ft. which is excellent in association with cherries or crab, for the white-striped branches and handsome autumn colour add interest when the others are out of flower.

The Paperbark Maple, *A. griseum,* when well grown in a sheltered position, is a magnificent spectacle. The divided leaves have a grey undertone throughout the summer and they contrast well with the polished orange bark. In October the leaves fall in a blaze of orange and scarlet.

I grow *A. japonicum aureum* surrounded with primroses in the spring, *Gentiana sino-ornata* for the autumn. Growth could be described as painfully slow, but when the garden is small this characteristic becomes a virtue. In spring the soft yellow of the leaves makes a patch of sunshine in the border while during the summer the green is relieved by an edging of red.

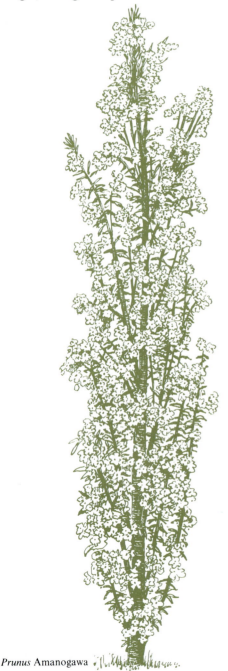

Prunus Amanogawa

Acer negundo variegatum has some virtues – it will put up with heavy soils, vicious winds, and with its silver-white variegated leaves brings colour to the border in the dankest of springs. Yet somehow this is not enough to make the Silver Maple a quality shrub. Cuttings taken in July, or better still in October root with alacrity.

Delicate and lovely, the Japanese Maples have a timelessness that makes even a young plant seem old, or contradictory though this may be, an old plant seem young. I certainly would not garden without them, for they will fit into any garden landscape from the ritualistic formality of a Japanese garden to the fresh flexibility of a heathered bank. Late spring frosts or a bitter east wind will scar the young leaves for the first few years after planting, so provide a shelter of quicker-growing shrubs to protect them, for all the virtue and garden worth of these trees is contained in their foliage. A soil which is acid or neutral in character seems to intensify the richness of autumn colouring. I remember an *A. palmatum* in full flame of autumn scarlet, planted around with the cool blue of aconitum, which made a serenely beautiful picture.

The earliest of many varieties to colour in autumn is *A. palmatum heptalobum osakazuki,* orange-scarlet against the silver of birch and pampas grass. Both this and the species grow slowly, very slowly with me, eventually to make trees 25 ft. high.

Autumn, though in glorious beauty my favourite season, is but a fleeting moment in time, so I prefer in a limited space to grow *A. palmatum atropurpureum,* with finely divided, bronze-purple leaves which delight me from bud burst until leaf fall. The acme of maple perfection is, undoubtedly, the finely divided leaves of *A. palmatum dissectum atropurpureum* which I grow surrounded by ferns and meconopsis. The setting sun will shine through the tree to turn the purple leaves to rich wine red.

The only method I have discovered other than grafting to propagate the Japanese maple is by air layering in April.

Aesculus

This genus will grow with amazing tolerance in the most inhospitable places. To see *Aesculus hippocastanum,* the Horse Chestnut beloved of all children, at a very beautiful best it must be planted in a wide grassed expanse. Then when the flower candles appear in spring against the burgeoning green of young growth, it is truly a picture to arrest attention. In the small garden it is a menace, robbing the soil and the light; a dull umbrella of foliage shadowing an arid waste where nothing else will grow.

Aesculus parviflora is better adapted to the small garden, making a spreading bush about 10 ft. across. Flowering in mid-August, it is particularly valuable with 8-in. trusses of either

Acer palmatum dissectum atropurpureum

Amelanchier canadensis

white or red flowers. The autumn colour is a warm soft yellow.

The Red Buckeye, *A. pavia,* will eventually make a bush 12 ft. high, but has the grace to flower when hardly out of the nursery. The dark red panicles of flower show colour in mid-July.

Ailanthus

Ailanthus altissima is frequently known by the common name of the Tree of Heaven, and I have often wondered why a tree with such doubtful claims to real beauty should be so honoured. That it is quick growing, tolerant of atmospheric pollution and possessed of large not unattractive leaves is undeniably true, but surely these qualities hardly warrant the sobriquet of Heavenly. In a quiet corner of the garden, with a wisteria-covered wall in the background, an ailanthus will add an air of rather oriental elegance and will provide shade under which even the planter will be able to sit in contemplation long before reaching his dotage.

It is propagated by root cuttings which are taken 3 to 4 in. long from the fleshy portion of the roots. The top is cut straight and the bottom on a slant so that there is no mistake when the pieces are lined out from the sand plunge in April.

Amelanchier

I grow amelanchiers from seed because not even in a mist unit will they condescend to root from cuttings with any degree of certainty. *Amelanchier canadensis,* the Shad Bush, comes very high on my list of indispensable shrubs. Even in winter the graceful form of the plant is obvious. In April each branch forms into a plethora of white blossom and the autumn leaf colour is pale yellow, deepening to copper red. In my garden it has taken 20 years for this splendid shrub to reach 14 ft. Where necessary, pruning, of which it shows a remarkable tolerance, should be aimed at emphasising the umbrella shape, and winter is the best time to perform this operation.

Amelanchier x *grandiflora* is a hybrid with *canadensis* as one parent. I prefer the pink-flowered form listed by some nurseries as *rubescens,* by others as *rosea.* Pink candyfloss would be an exact description of this bush in full bloom, the autumn colour of the leaves being a rich deep red.

Andromeda

Andromeda polifolia compacta could hardly be called versatile for it demands an acid peaty soil. The grey leaves with clusters of bright pink flowers from May onwards, sometimes into July, make this a splendid ground cover plant. I mulch the bed each year so that the branches root themselves to spread the group wider.

Aralia

Aralia elata, or as it is sometimes called *A. chinensis,* is a shrub I have a complex about. In winter the straight, branchless stems thickly studded with thorns resemble devils' walking sticks. Once the compound leaves, which are 3 to 4 ft. long by 18 in. wide, unfold, it becomes a flower arranger's delight. In due season, usually around August, these are surmounted by huge panicles of white flowers. The uninhibited freedom with which this shrub suckers makes control, rather than propagation, a problem. Suckers dug away in early spring find a welcome in gardens of fellow enthusiasts. In the various soils I have grown it in, from clay to sand, it has never reached more than 14 ft. high.

Arbutus

Though a member of the *ericaceae,* this genus shows a benign tolerance of alkaline soils. One of the finest specimens of the Strawberry Tree, *Arbutus unedo,* I have ever seen grows in a lime soil, full in the path of a wind from the sea. My plant merits and receives rather more consideration, making a rounded mound of delightful greenery throughout the year. The panicles of white flowers which open in late autumn are quickly followed by the 'strawberry' fruits so that a few of both may be seen at the same time giving this shrub a very cheerful demeanour. I once tasted the fruit expecting acidity, but disappointingly found that there was no real flavour at all.

Seed sown immediately it is ripe offers the best means of increasing stock. I have not found pruning necessary except when a branch is damaged by snow or reckless driving with the wheelbarrow.

Aronia

Six years ago I bought some holly and rhododendron to brighten up a bed of bamboo in the autumn, and at the same time I also bought an

Aronia arbutifolia

Aronia arbutifolia. Though only reaching a height of 3 ft. in the first year, by mid-September it looked as if someone had lighted a fire in the border for the leaves coloured scarlet, orange, and yellow. Greatly encouraged, I have now added colchicum bulbs to complete the picture in cool purple and white. My specimen spreads by self-layering, but very restrainedly, and shows no particular preference to soil or even degree of exposure. However, I have found the autumn colour is better in part shade.

Arundinaria

The bamboo family is made up of several genera but for convenience I have grouped them all under the title arundinaria. *Arundinaria anceps* is a species so rampant that it is only suitable for the large garden where it will grow 9 ft. high. The canes are green and they are topped with glossy green leaves. As a child I cut the canes to use as 'props' in Indian raids or big game hunts while my father, more prosaically I thought, cut them for plant stakes.

Arundinaria murielae came to me by mistake as the species *nitida* – a perchance which normally would have aroused me to wrath and indignation. Fortunately, I did not discover the fact until the bright green young canes made an appearance and by this time the plant had so impressed me with its graceful elegance that removing even a single cane would have been a desecration. Again the long arching canes will reach 7 to 9 ft. and as they are not prone to suckering this bamboo will make a fine specimen plant for a lawn. *A. nitida* has purple-coloured canes and a rather neater foliage than *murielae* but is in other respects identical. Of all the bamboos this is the species I like the best.

Arundinaria viridistriata with yellow and green leaves is a most unpredictable species. In the garden near Clitheroe, Lancashire, which provided my plants they grew in open woodland and the canes were 3 ft. high. Each year they were scythed in swathes to encourage young growth which produces the best foliage. I suspect that the garden's need of bonfire ash was also a reason. In my garden they shot up to 4 ft., the foliage was tatterdemalion-like and altogether different from the parents. Possibly a permanently wet soil could have been the trouble.

The bamboos belonging to the genus *phyllostachys* have not accepted Harlow Car quite so

Arundinaria nitida

posedly edible shoots. The canes fade to a straw yellow and the foliage is dark green and luxuriant. Like *A. nitida,* this is a splendid variety for planting as a lawn specimen.

Aucuba

Aucuba japonica offers a shining example of vegetable good nature, because if ever a shrub was called upon to perform miracles the Spotted Laurel could certainly be so described. In the black grime of city cemeteries, their leaves thick with soot, they are condemned to a sunless well nigh airless existence, a picture of woe and neglect. Give the plant reasonable growing conditions with a proper mixture of male and female varieties, so that in due season the bushes are festooned with scarlet berries, and the real quality of the shrub is obvious. *A. japonica variegata* is the form most commonly seen struggling to survive in some city plot; *hillieri* is a green-leaved form which looks extremely becoming in full berry but *nana rotundifolia* is my favourite with a neat habit and scarlet berries. Cuttings taken in August – September root so easily I have never tried sowing seeds, which is an alternative method of propagation.

Berberis

Many gardens would look ill furnished in places were it not for the large selection of berberis available. Most of the really desirable species will succeed in a wide range of soils, growing in sun or partial shade. The early plantings made at Harlow Car had to take the full force of the wind across the valley, so they must be possessed of iron hard constitutions. I have never noticed the birds rejecting the fruit of any varieties except those of *Berberis aggregata.* The genus includes a wide range of dwarf and tall, evergreen and deciduous shrubs which I plunder unashamedly to add grace to my garden. Whenever I wish to increase this family, a search around the parent bushes usually reveals many self-sown seedlings.

Berberis aggregata makes a dense, intensely thorny bush which, by the sheer beauty of its contribution to autumn colour, must surely be one of the best deciduous species. The masses of bright scarlet berries almost hide the rich red-purple of the dying leaves. Buccaneer and

readily as the arundinarias, a fact which causes regret as they are very handsome, and do not spread all over the garden.

Phyllostachys aurea, whose shoots are said to be edible, has pale cream canes but rather non-descript foliage. *P. nigra* grew wonderfully well in the gardens where I worked in Norfolk and Cornwall, possibly because it enjoys sunshine and a fairly dry root run. The canes of *nigra boryana* are mottled green and black and the shadow patterns cast by the rather dense foliage complete the jungle effect. My first choice, however, would be *nigra henonis* though this would not include attempting to eat the sup-

Aucuba japonica variegata

Pirate King differ from the type only in that they are more erect in habit.

Berberis buxifolia and its slow-growing variety *nana* could be utilised as rock garden plants. The dark green leaves are silver underneath and the flowers which appear in early spring would make a better impression if they were carried clear of the leaves.

Berberis darwinii must be one of the loveliest of evergreen flowering shrubs. Usually it makes a bush 8 ft. high and is covered in late April with a mass of rich orange-yellow pompon flowers. I

Berberis darwinii

have a plant on a wall and all the year round the small holly-like leaves soften the masonry. The flowering is profuse under the shelter of the wall, while in autumn the berries hang like luscious black grapes, much to the delight of the birds which reside in the garden.

Berberis dictyophylla came to me as a chance seedling in a box of mixed shrubs. The plant is now 4 ft. high, the young shoots scarlet but covered with a grey bloom. In the autumn the leaves are absolutely delightful, first green rimmed scarlet which deepens until the whole leaf is bright silver and red. *B.* x *irwinii* will always be represented in person in my garden, or by one of its numerous offspring, for they rank with the choicest shrubs. The type is a dwarf bush, 3 ft. high, with arching branches. The flowers, which are crimson in bud and orange-yellow when they open, appear in April. The variety *coccinea* is a pearl – tight, compact, and very prim with flowers of coral red, while *corallina compacta* always reminds me of a garden in the Lake District, quiet under a warm April sun, with the berberis making a flame of vivid scarlet against the white limestone rock. Few places are lovelier than White Cragg Garden in the spring and it is well worth a visit if you are ever in Westmorland.

Berberis linearifolia has an almost tropical air and the gayest orange-red flowers imaginable. I have six plants in a rather exposed position, and they positively light up a cold April day when in full bloom.

With *B. darwinii* as one parent and *B. linearifolia* the other, what else could the off-spring, *lologensis,* be but superb. The habit is erect and the evergreen leaves well formed, while the flowers are yellow, softened with a hint of peach.

Berberis x *stenophylla* must take after *B. empetrifolia,* for it bears no resemblance whatsoever to *darwinii,* the other parent. It is an elegant, graceful shrub with long arching branches wreathed in April with yellow, sweetly scented flowers. I give it plenty of room to expand its full charm, then tip the branches which adventure too far immediately the flowers fade. Sucker shoots, which appear around the parent shrub, are easily detached when fresh stocks are needed.

Berberis thunbergii lacks the flamboyance of its varietal forms *atropurpurea* and *atropurpurea nana* which have coloured leaves throughout the summer. In spite of this deficiency it is a superb shrub of compact habit. The yellow flowers in spring followed by the bright red berries, and deep scarlet of autumn colour make this species one of the choicest barberries. Where garden space is limited I would choose the variety *atropurpurea.* Used as a centrepiece in a blue and white ground planting, or as a contrast with deep orange annuals, it is charmingly effective.

Finally, having ignored the vast legions of berberis worthy of notice but not of the elect, to *B. wilsoniae,* a dwarf shrublet only 2 to 3 ft. high. The tiny grey-green leaves in autumn turn deep red, as if to vie with the orange-scarlet of the fruit. Judging by the way the rabbits haunt this impenetrable tangle of branches I have often wondered if this is the original thorn bush Brer Fox pitched Brer Rabbit into.

There will be enough self-sown seedlings of *B. wilsoniae* to satisfy all but the Fagans of the gardening world. A selected form listed as Bountiful may have virtues in excess of those possessed by the parent, but I can not discover them. A modest percentage of cuttings taken in September with a heel of old wood can be relied on to root. So tolerant are most berberis yet withal so attractive that I use them to create shelter for less hardy specimens.

Betula

No tree excites more affection in me than the graceful native birch. In winter sculptural in white beauty, in spring touched with the pale green charm of breaking bud, then in autumn all golden glory in the October sunshine. First *Betula platyphylla japonica,* the ghostly Japanese White Birch, a fine specimen tree up to 40 ft. high. I trim away the lower branches so that the white stem can be seen to full advantage. I saw the Western Chinese form, *B. platyphylla szechuanica* for the first time over a 3-acre expanse of lawn, the wide sweeping branches a graceful crown to the white column of the bole. Almost any soil seems suitable, they grow well on the heavy clay soil here, but may be shorter lived than those which flourish on a sandy soil.

Betula papyrifera is the Canoe Birch and it brings much the same effect to the garden as our own native birch. The varietal form from Alaska, *kenaica,* has a bark which glows a warm orange and this together with a rather upright habit makes it suitable for planting in a restricted space.

Betula pendula, silver birch, the graceful lady of the woods has given rise to several varietal forms, none more elegant than the type plant. Every day of the year my work takes me at least once amongst groves of indigenous birch and always, at all seasons, they are lovely. Some have thrown up four or five stems, as a result of being damaged in youth, instead of just one, and these are without doubt the most picturesque. Now I plant seedlings in the nursery, head them back to ground level, thin the shoots to 3 or 5 as they break and have miniature groves all ready as needed. The variety *youngii* or Youngs' Weeping Birch is far better in small plots especially town gardens than the often planted *Salix alba tristis.*

Propagation of *B. pendula* is readily achieved by means of seed, except with the variety *youngii* where recourse has to be made to budding or grafting.

Buddleia

Buddleias should be planted in every garden where there are children for warm sunshine will bring out the honey scent of the flowers and youngsters can enjoy watching the rich collection of insects which make haste to the banquet. *Buddleia alternifolia* from China makes a tall shrub with long arching branches, covered in July with lilac-purple, delicately fragrant flowers. A little judicious thinning of the branches improves the shape of the bush enormously. Cuttings taken in July or August root readily in a sandy compost.

Buddleia davidii is not really a landscape plant, and should not be given a too prominent place in the border. When hard pruned, as it must be to keep it within reasonable bounds, it presents an appearance strongly reminiscent of a badly finished hat stand. Apart from the typical intolerance the genus invariably shows for bad drainage, it will make an effort to grow on most soils. The pruning back to between 3 and 9 buds of the previous year's growth is performed in March. Of the many varieties listed, Black Knight with deep violet flowers makes a striking picture against a grey background. Royal Red, when thinned to only 3 or 5 branches, yields the most enormous panicles of dark red flowers, which border on the verge of vulgarity. Fascinating and Charming are two which could be properly described as pink while White Bouquet and White Cloud, as the names imply, supply a patch of white to relieve the bolder colours. Cuttings will root at any time during the growing season.

The Orange Ball Tree, *B. globosa,* is altogether too gaunt and straggling to be pleasant. In June when covered with globose orange flowers it has a brief beauty but in my opinion it is not worth the 12 months ground rent needed.

Buddleia alternifolia

Buddleia davidii

Amelanchier canadensis has shared garden space with me for over twenty years. A delight to the eye in spring with racemes of white flowers, then in autumn it becomes a carnival as the leaves turn first pale gold then copper red.

That some bamboo are invasive weeds has earned the whole family a bad name, *Arundinaria japonica* provides an oriental theme without bidding to take over the whole garden.

Camellias look especially lovely when used as wall plants in a courtyard garden. These are the beautiful flowers of *Camellia japonica elegans*.

Callicarpa giraldiana

Callicarpa

Callicarpa giraldiana is enjoying a sudden burst of respect now that it has been discovered by the flower arrangers. I have grown it for 14 years in a secluded corner where it has made a modest bush 3 ft. high. In the summer it goes unnoticed but as the leaves turn soft rose pink and the bright lilac, seemingly artificial berries appear, the charm becomes more assertive. Good drainage and an extra ration of potash as well as the fish fertiliser all my shrubs expect each year, are small recompense for the rather unusual contribution this shrub makes to the panoply of autumn.

Calluna

I find it easy to become almost lyrical about the ling of our Yorkshire moors. Indeed, were the garden around my house left to nature, the patches of heathers from the moors nearby would soon creep back in. Gloriously informal and lending themselves to most planting schemes providing the soil is acid, they really are plants which thrive on the minimum of attention. Dress the soil liberally with peat or well-rotted organic matter, then plant deeply, to the extent of leaving only the tips of the shoots showing.

After flowering trim the spikes hard back to encourage a bushy habit.

There must be easily 150 varieties to choose from but the following are those which give me most pleasure. *Calluna vulgaris alba pilosa,* 10 in. high with white flowers over pale foliage; *alportii* with crimson flowers on long spikes, good for cutting; Darkness, compact, with thick spikes of dark red flowers; and H. E. Beale and Peter Sparkes so very much alike with their double pink flowers, but so very essential in the shrub border or heather garden. Robert Chapman, I grow for the clear gold foliage, surrounded in summer by *Gentiana macaulayi,* while a good white to bring luck is Mair's Variety. A few lichen-covered boulders add the final touch of authenticity, with here and there a conifer.

Cuttings of side shoots taken in August root easily in compost of peat and sand made up in the sun frame. For limited quantities layering is labour saving and always meets with success.

Camellia

Sooner or later the beginner is tempted by the very romance of the name to plant a representative of this genus. I succumbed some 20 years ago, and long since transferred my allegiance to rhododendrons as easily the best flowering evergreens. However, where suitable shelter from cutting east winds or late frost can be given they do make a lovely show, for though reasonably hardy in leaf, the flower buds are easily damaged. Like the rhododendrons they positively decline any but an acid soil which is rich in organic matter, leafmould, or peat. Except in the most favoured localities it is wiser to concentrate on varieties of *Camellia japonica* such as Adolphe Audusson, blood red, semi double; *donckelarii,* large crimson blooms flecked with white; *elegans,* deep peach pink, very large; and Lady Clare which is soft pink and although its rather spreading branches are often damaged under heavy snow, it is lovely as a wall plant.

Donation is listed as a variety of *C. x williamsii,* but it has all the toughness of a full blooded *japonica.* This is decidedly my favourite camellia and the glorious peach-pink flowers nearly rival the best rhododendrons.

Cuttings of semi-ripened wood taken in July root in pumice or a peat and sand compost. As an alternative method of propagation, layering is usually successful.

Caragana arborescens

Caragana

Caragana arborescens, the Pea Tree, is worth inclusion in the shrub border on foliage effect alone. The finely cut, compound leaves turn soft primrose yellow with the first frost of autumn and the typically pea-shaped flowers, which begin to appear in June, are also a good yellow. A free-draining soil is advisable, for though caragana will grow in wet clay it makes a much smaller shrub than the normal 15 ft. and it is rather short lived.

Cuttings taken with a heel of old wood in mid-August can be persuaded to root without much difficulty, but seed is far easier and more interesting. I discovered this by accident 8 years ago, when a single sowing of caragana seed eventually produced some vigorously upright bushes, another flat topped and spreading and yet another which stubbornly refused to grow more than 4 ft. high.

Caragana pygmaea is my favourite, and the longest lived with me at 16 years old. At first glance it resembles a sparse-leaved heather but in May the slender shoots are decorated with delicate pale gold pendant blossoms. Once again seed is the best method of propagation.

Carpenteria

There are some shrubs suitable for neither my soil nor climate which I still persist in trying to grow. Even now the sixth specimen of *Carpenteria californica* ekes out a forlornly miserable existence in a corner under the south wall. In Devon, Birmingham, and Dolgellau, Merioneth, I have seen this beautiful evergreen 6 ft. high, smothered in pure white, golden-stamened flowers like drifted snow at the foot of a wall. Given the two essentials of a well-drained soil and a wall facing full south this very choice evergreen should succeed. Ladham's Variety is said to be freer flowering, but the specimen I grew was certainly no hardier than the type. Layering suitably placed branches in autumn or cuttings made into a frame in August are reliable methods of ensuring a reserve of young plants.

Carpinus

Carpinus betulus, the common hornbeam, languishes in the shadow of the beech, but as acquaintance ripens it becomes a tree of considerable character. Some trees one can pass every day and they are still no more than just a piece of wood with branches. However, few people can dismiss a hornbeam in so casual a fashion. As a hedging plant beech is acknowledged as the superior, for only when clipping is done in July and August will the hornbeam retain its leaves for the winter.

The tallest tree I know is 50 ft. high; an impressive sight in winter with the fluted trunk a picture of rugged strength. For those with limited space the variety *fastigiata* makes a delightful pyramidal small tree.

Caryopteris

Any shrub which combines blue flowers with grey, slightly aromatic foliage must be worthy of inclusion in even the most select planting

Caryopteris x *clandonensis*

The blue flowers and grey foliage of *Caryopteris* x *clandonensis* have an illusory quality, like a wisp of smoke in the border during September. A green or gold background emphasises their delicate charm.

The catalpa or Indian Bean Tree has such a presence it is best viewed uncluttered by other vegetation. The large leaves with panicles of foxglove-like flowers erupting through them in midsummer are a memorable sight.

OPPOSITE: The soft powder blue of the ceanothus provides the perfect colour contrast to the orange flowers of *Eccremocarpus scaber*.

schemes. I grow *Caryopteris* x *clandonensis* against a wall and, because it is not to be trusted outdoors in a really hard winter, I take cuttings each autumn. My bushes never grow more than 3 ft. high but maybe this is because I plant five specimens close together and the overall effect is quite handsome. Of the soil, it would be sufficient to say *Iris stylosa* grows in the same well-drained bed which is deprived of excess moisture by an overhanging roof and is baked by all the sun our unpredictable weather will vouchsafe.

Cassinia

The golden heather of New Zealand, *Cassinia fulvida,* though mediocre in flower makes a very good looking foliage shrub. I planted five nearly fifteen years ago and so far only one has died and the tallest is now 6 ft. The leaves crowded together with the undercolouring of copper are especially conspicuous in spring. Cuttings taken with a heel in September root easily in a cold frame.

Catalpa

I knew catalpa as a child by the name of Spanish Saddle – a name which for some reason was forgotten long ago. It makes a low spreading tree with large soft-textured leaves. *Catalpa bignonioides,* the delightful Indian Bean Tree, has panicles of white flowers flecked with purple and yellow usually in August. The wood is extremely brittle and is liable to fracture under heavy snow or strong winds. However, the scars are soon hidden by the fresh young shoots which break around the cut surface. A well-drained, rather poor soil is quite suitable.

The golden-leaved form *aurea* in spite of affectionate care refuses to honour me, an insult rendered more intolerable by the fact that in a garden nearby a specimen treated with contempt grows happily only to be plundered for background foliage to flower arrangements. *C. speciosa* has the same brittle wood as *bignonioides* but the leaves are larger and heart shaped whilst the flowers, which are white spotted with purple, are carried in panicles during July. Eventually it will make a large but rather attractively shaped tree.

Ceanothus

Ceanothus includes species with popular names redolent of romance – Californian Lilac, Jersey Tea, and Squaw Carpet. I find it a matter of great regret that not even with the deciduous species can I sit back and enjoy that rare delight of a shrub covered in blue flowers for no sooner do the ceanothus in my garden reach full size than along comes a really severe late frost to turn fresh green to black ruin. This is just one of the penalties paid for a glorious view of the Pennines in my over-exposed garden.

Both the evergreen and deciduous species need a hot sun-baked position and a light free-draining soil to really flourish, so on a clay soil put them against the south or west wall of the house or any other sheltered location with the roots in a carefully prepared compost.

A. T. Johnson is an evergreen bush with a crop of blue flowers in spring followed by a repeat display in autumn. It is lovely in combination with chaenomeles. *Ceanothus* Autumnal Blue, as the name implies, flowers in late August through to September. Delight was splendid in my garden for 5 years, then was caught in growth by a late frost. The flowers, in long panicles, are dainty and a good crisp blue. This hybrid is generally one of the hardiest.

Gloire de Versailles, a deciduous bush, presents a rather stiff formal appearance but the powder-blue flowers are extremely pleasant in late summer. *C.* x *veitchianus* (I have mine labelled Brilliant) is a neat bush and in my garden the blue flowers open with those of the yellow-blossomed shrub rose, *Rosa cantabrigiensis.* *Ceanothus prostratus,* Squaw Carpet, which I grew in a rock garden scree for 9 years, is a lovely creeping shrub with blue flowers which start to appear in May and continue into June.

Pruning of the evergreens, so far as I am concerned, consists of removing frost-damaged twigs down to sound wood, or in the case of Gloire de Versailles, once a framework of mature growth is established, spurring young growth back as necessary. Cuttings root into a cold frame when taken in August, or better still into a heated propagating frame in July.

Ceratostigma

Ceratostigma willmottianum takes the very sensible precaution of becoming herbaceous

Ceratostigma willmottianum

Chaenomeles

in severe winters. The first time this happened I assumed the worst, and was just about to plant a very expensive replacement in the same position when I noticed bright scarlet buds poking through the soil, which on investigation proved to be the timorous ceratostigma. The blue flowers with a warmth which reminds me of *Gentiana verna,* open in July, while the foliage turns a good deep red in autumn. My bushes are never much more than 3 ft. in height making just the right companion for the glaucous-leaved rue.

Cercis

Cercis siliquastrum always looks in need of a thorough spring clean to me. Even when the branches are clothed during June in lilac-purple flowers I still take a somewhat jaundiced view of a tree most gardeners revere. The best specimens I have ever seen grew on a lime soil over gravel and were especially attractive, so the proud owners told me, as the seed pods ripened to a blue-tinted green.

Chaenomeles

The ebullient, irrepressable *Chaenomeles japonica* is dazzling in flower, cheerfully ugly the rest of the year. I would always have one plant about the place somewhere but I prefer them trained onto a wall. By pruning back the young

growth right through the summer a mass of plump flower buds are formed the full length of the spurs.

In spite of its name, *C. japonica* Boule de Feu has apricot blooms flecked with orange. I think the ultimate height can be little more than 3 ft. as my specimen has taken 8 years to grow 30 in. *C. speciosa atrococcinea* shows more ambition, the flowers deep crimson on branches topping 5 ft.

Chaenomeles speciosa nivalis is a good white form but it must be summer pruned or the colour is hidden by a mass of leaves. Personally I would prefer the hybrid between the two species under the title *C.* x *superba* Knap Hill Scarlet which is a fiery combination of orange and scarlet holding a torch for spring in every petal during April.

Chaenomeles speciosa simonii is a plant of exceptional character, compact and tidy in all its parts with the flat semi-double blood-red blooms having a camellia-like quality.

Soil type does not seem to be particularly important, but I give my plants a sun-soaked place and they love it. A little extra potash is well rewarded with hard-petalled flowers in profusion.

Chimonanthus

Chimonanthus praecox is a shrub whose popular name Winter Sweet suggests an eagerness to

Shrubs with blue flowers are always a welcome addition, particularly those obliging enough to flower in October. A warm sunny corner suits *Ceratostigma willmottıanum* and even in such a situation top growth dies down to soil level in winter.

Cistus x *purpureus* will accept with relish the hottest, driest place the garden affords. It revels in the sunlight with a charming succession of silk-textured flowers.

A carpet of bluebells
adds a misty undertone
to a specimen tree of
Cornus florida rubra in
full bloom. The leaves
are red tinged in spring
and colour well in the
autumn.

Cytisus x *praecox*
becomes a cascade of
yellow flowers during
April and looks well in
the company of
aubrieta and *Alyssum
saxatile* which flower at
the same time.

please, which experience proves to be utterly incorrect. Indeed, the plant is miffish in the extreme, flowering indifferently on one soil, yet in the next plot burgeoning into pale yellow, sweetly scented flowers all down the leafless branches in March. A hot sun-baked position in a well-drained, rather starved soil seems to be most suitable. By shortening back the season's growths to 4 or 5 buds in August and giving a dressing of high potash fertiliser, reluctant prima donnas can often be persuaded to bring forth something more than a travesty of blossom.

Choisya

Choisya ternata is an elegant glossy-leaved evergreen which in early spring exhibits the delicately fragrant, creamy-white flowers which earn it the name of Mexican Orange Blossom. It should be planted near a much-used path or door where

Clethra alnifolia

there is shelter and a free-draining soil so that the distillation can be enjoyed when mild weather persuades blossoming.

Cuttings of semi-ripened wood taken in July – August root easily in a sand frame. The only pruning I do is to remove damaged shoots.

Cistus

The rock roses are Mediterranean shrubs which like light, free-draining soil and a warm sunny position. Three varieties of those tried in my garden lived seven years, and cuttings taken from them continue to grace the garden in a sheltered bed by the house. *Cistus* x *corbariensis,* with olive-green leaves and in due season crimson buds which open to pure white flowers, is an aromatic shrub of quality. *C.* x *cyprius* is a splendid hybrid, which at 6 ft. is taller by 18 in. than *corbariensis* with each white petal stained at the base with deep scarlet. I prefer *C. laurifolius* to all others because it lingers longer in my company. The flowers are creamy white deepening to yellow at the base. Had I a paved terrace with sheltering walls then I would grow hybrids like *C.* x *purpureus* with flowers of rosy crimson blotched brown, or better still Silver Pink or even *ladaniferus* to cheer the July days with Mediterranean flamboyance.

Cuttings taken more or less at any time during

Choisya ternata

Cistus x *cyprius*

the growing season, or seed, will ensure a creditable increase for effort expended.

Clethra

Clethra alnifolia should be more widely grown. It is not fastidious except in the question of soil which must be free of any hint of lime. It associates contentedly with rhododendrons and in September, as the pulse of the garden slows, the cream-white spiked trusses open and fill the air for some distance with a delicate fragrance. Avoid only the form listed as *rosea,* a villainous washed-out pink, hideous to behold and parsimonious in producing flowers.

Pruning is accepted with equanimity even when amateurishly performed by rabbits, cows and a very unpredictable rotary grass cutter. Propagation can be by cuttings or layering, whichever is more convenient.

Cornus

Cornus alba has proved a worthy friend which when planted as a windbreak spreads, each branch rooting where it touches the ground, into a dense mass of shoots. For the connoisseur, *C. alba sibirica,* with brilliant scarlet shoots in winter, and less vigorous enthusiasm to colonise the whole garden, is better value. *C. alba spaethii* is the supreme champion because the golden variegated leaves spread cheer on the dampest day in summer and like the type plant it can really cover the ground, a veritable racehorse of a plant.

Cornus florida rarely condescends to vouchsafe more than a brief selection of the white petal-like bracts with which it delights all who see it growing wild in North America, although I am permitted to enjoy the rich autumn colouring. About 8 ft. is the most plants here have attained after 17 years. The form known as *rubra* is only a travesty of red. Could the blush be heightened by a degree then its charm might rival that of the type plant. *C. stolonifera* had a rather poor start in my garden as it inadvertently moved within the sphere of influence of a large fire. It has completely recovered, however, and is throwing out suckers and spreading rapidly to fill a corner of the peat garden. The dark red shoots are best viewed from a nearby path with the sun behind them. *C. s. flaviramea* has yellow-barked young shoots which are attractive when grown with the type plant and the Whitewashed Bramble, *Rubus cockburnianus. C. mas* shows no reluctance whatever to grow, and after 16 years has topped the 9-ft. mark here. The angular branch outline is pleasant in winter for the plant is deciduous, then in February every twig burgeons forth in a multitude of yellow pompon flowers. Varieties like *elegantissima* and *variegata* are useful and attractive variations of the type plant.

Daphne cneorum is a mound of pink-scented fragrance through April into May. It is a choice shrub for a sun-baked ledge in the rock garden or a corner of the border.

The arching branches of *Deutzia* x *rosea carminea* are festooned with delicate rose-carmine tinted flowers in June.

The gold and green variegated leaves of *Elaeagnus pungens maculata* on a sunny winter's day warm the eye. This is one of the very choice evergreen shrubs.

The fruits of the spindle tree, *Euonymus europaeus*, are extremely decorative and much sought after by floral artists. The orange seeds contrast with the scarlet capsules as they ripen and split.

Corylopsis spicata

Corylopsis

Corylopsis pauciflora has the precocious habit of flowering in March – April. Fortunately we are often granted a few mild, sun-blessed days in which to appreciate the delicate fragrance of the drooping racemes of yellow flowers. Incidently, they make worthy pot plants but rarely exceed 36 in. even outside.

Corylopsis spicata is taller and with me somewhat hardier than *C. pauciflora*. In appearance it is very like a hamamelis or hazel, the 5-in. spikes of yellow flowers are deliciously scented, opening mid-April. I planted one specimen near a flight of well-used steps and for 5 years it has given pleasure to all who pass by when it is in bloom.

Pruning is only required if the twigs are nipped by frost, otherwise leave well alone. To increase my collection I find layering the most fruitful method, cutting a low branch back hard, then pegging down the young shoots which break from the stump.

Corylus

I purchased *Corylus avellana contorta,* the Corkscrew Hazel, after reading E. A. Bowles description of it growing in what he dubbed his Lunatic Asylum. The branches are twisted in the most remarkable manner, and have a curious beauty when hung with catkins in March. Two coloured-leaved hazels, the yellow cobnut and purple-leaved filbert have never appealed to me. For flower arrangers the plants may have special appeal.

Grafting or budding are the only methods of propagation that I have found really successful.

Cotinus

Cotinus coggygria is a horribly garbled substitute for a name to replace the simplicity of *Rhus cotinus*. The Venetian Sumach, or more descriptive still the Smoke Tree, from the Caucasus is a joy to behold each autumn when the leaves turn red under the billowing steel grey of the inflorescences. I like them best against a dark green background, the sunlight broken by foliage, making a pattern of light and shade on the brilliant colours.

A freely drained, yet moisture-retentive soil encourages the vigorous growth which in mature specimens can reach 8 to 10 ft. The coloured-leaved forms I have grown include *foliis purpureis* with leaves of rich purple which look gorgeous when planted round with white colchicum. I hard prune the branches in spring which helps to intensify the shades of the leaves, and keeps the shrub compact. Notcutts is a form with dark red leaves which need sunshine to light them up or they appear dull black.

My method of propagation is to remove pieces as required from the parent plant with a sharp spade. Possibly it would be simpler to dig the whole lot up and divide it but this puts all the shrub in jeopardy and I never need more than one piece at a time.

Cotoneaster

Ranging as they do from species which grow only inches high to tree-like specimens of 20 ft. or so, cotoneasters are virtually indispensable to the gardener. The choice is bewildering, and there is space here only to include those which have proved their worth in my experience.

Cotoneaster adpressus praecox has arching branches and grows up to 18 in. high. I use it to give height in one corner of my rock garden. The small leaves turn scarlet in autumn, but unfortunately the orange berries parade a very brief glory before the birds eat them.

Cotoneaster bullatus is in itself a gem of a species, but it is overshadowed by a selected form called *floribundus*. The large deeply veined leaves and clusters of dark berries make a picture to warm the heart. Unfortunately, they also warm the stomachs of every passing bird, so make the most of the presentation while it lasts. At least the red and purple of the dying leaves remains after the gourmets fly on. Some books have this plant as tall growing but my specimen would hardly win any prizes in this speed mad world.

Cotoneaster conspicuus is a graceful, small-leaved shrub with arching wide-spreading branches. The white flowers are followed by equally numerous bright red berries. *C.* x *cornubia* grows 20 ft. high with the largest berries of all and looks most effective when grown as a standard. I lost two before it occurred to me that the plant hated wet feet even more than I do. It is important therefore to make certain that all surplus moisture drains away rapidly.

There are a large number of cotoneasters growing in the garden outside my house. For a long time I gave the accolade to a species labelled *wardii* because it was planted in the most efficacious position for display of the silver-grey leaves and orange berries. Then I was given another *C. wardii* from an unimpeachable source, and now I find the original plant is *C. franchetii sternianus*. Those who buy a plant should place it so that the rising sun shines full upon rime-frosted leaves.

Without a doubt, *C. horizontalis* is the most widely used member of the genus. From traffic islands in the middle of the city to farmhouse walls in the countryside, it exhibits the characteristic pattern of branches in autumn, scarlet of leaf, orange of berry, always a model of decorous beauty. Planted against a wall, with a little training, it builds tier upon tier of branches to soften the aridity of the masonry. Cuttings, self-layered branches, or seeds make propagation almost child's play.

Cotoneaster microphyllus thymifolius is hard, ground hugging and rather like wire netting with leaves on. Planted in the rock garden it will follow and emphasise every rock and contour in a splendidly affectionate way.

Cotoneaster nitens is especially desirable for

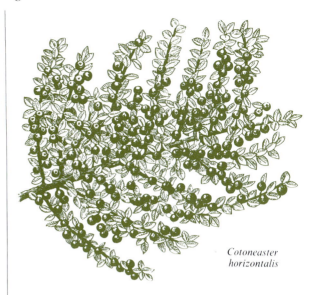

Cotoneaster horizontalis

the beauty of the leaf colour in autumn, particularly when planted around with *Lilium speciosum*.

Tall and elegant, the matriarch to a tribe of hybrids, *C. salicifolius* has pendulous branches which are encrusted in autumn with a mass of scarlet berries in the manner of an oriental curtain. It makes a fine specimen for border or lawn.

C. salicifolius fructu-luteo berries furiously in my garden with big luscious fruits which are wax like in their creamy opaqueness – a gift to those who delight in the unusual.

Last then to the queen, *C. salicifolius flocossus*, narrowly columnar, the branches sweep the ground clothed in slender leaves which are hidden in October by masses of small red berries. If you grow *floccosus* then you must partner it with a cluster of Silver Queen pampas grass.

Self-sown seedlings abound from cotoneaster, all are saved, then if found wanting, discarded.

Crataegus

I have a thorn hedge around my garden and just outside the front gate there are standard forms both weeping and normal. There is also even a tiny pygmy on top of the rock garden. As much at home in the bustling city as a mountain glen the thorn is the starling of the shrub world.

Undoubtedly it would be easy to lose space and time amongst the species but none have the character of our two indigenous thorns.

Crataegus monogyna turns the hedgerows and coppices all over the Yorkshire Dales into billow-

The witch hazels are
invaluable winter-
flowering shrubs with
fragrant yellow flowers
along leafless branches
in January and
February. In some,
notably *Hamamelis* x
intermedia, the leaves
colour attractively, as
illustrated, above a
carpet of autumn
gentian.

Hebe Autumn Glory is
a beautiful, late-
flowering dwarf shrub.
I like the flowers best
when grown intermixed
with those of *Calluna
vulgaris* H. E. Beale or
Peter Sparkes.

OPPOSITE: The gay
yellow cascades of
forsythia in full bloom
under the warm
benevolence of April
sunshine are an integral
part of spring.

ing waves of white blossom in May and is equally lovely in October when covered in a multitude of crimson berries.

I grow the Glastonbury Thorn, *C. monogyna praecox* (sometimes listed in catalogues as *biflora*). Some years it leafs up much earlier than others while *C. m. inermis compacta,* which graces my rock garden, is a stiff impregnable shrublet 3 ft. high and 14 years old. Flowers and berries are yielded, but in moderate quantities. *C. m. pendula rosea* is a pleasant weeping tree with pink flowers but on a heavy soil it needs staking for at least three years. The ultimate height will be around 18 ft. *C. m. fastigiata* (*stricta*) is a useful small tree for a limited space if one positively demands a thorn, but there are better looking trees.

Crataegus oxyacantha has sported to give a wider choice. Standards should be avoided on exposed sites with poorly drained soil. The trees get top heavy and the root development, restricted by soil condition, is incapable of supporting them and the wind plays havoc. *C. o. coccinea plena,* the widely planted Double Crimson Thorn or Paul's Double Scarlet has a lot to commend it. Plant a double white variety as well so that the branches run together, and let a blue clematis wind through to mingle blue with white. The single scarlet *punicea* I like planted around with heather and yellow broom.

The height of all the above when fully grown is between 20 and 25 ft. Propagation of named varieties is by grafting on to seedling stocks, or by budding in July.

Cytisus

I like to grow cytisus from seed as they flower when two or three years old and there is the joy of anticipation, not knowing what the colours are likely to be. The White Spanish Broom, *Cytisus albus,* has been a source of pleasure to me for years. It flowers profusely, has a graceful habit, and can be relied on to suffer most soils unless they are waterlogged. The ultimate height is about 8 ft. and, as with all brooms, the young shoots should be clipped over after flowering to keep the stems furnished to ground level.

Cytisus battandieri is a splendid plant for a high wall where the sun can cook the wood in a somewhat pale imitation of the warmth of its native Morocco. Given perfect drainage and a rather arid soil, the grey leaves with their silver

Cytisus battandieri

sheen make a good foil to the conical clusters of yellow, pineapple-scented flowers. The tallest specimen I have seen grew in boiler ashes to a height of 15 ft.

I grow *C. nigricans* round a silver fir. Its sparsely leaved, slender shoots which are up to 3 ft. high are adorned with yellow flowers and they open in succession for several weeks in late summer.

One of the earliest to flower in April is *C. x praecox,* a lovely ghost of a plant when covered in pale cream flowers and excellent in association with the hybrid heaths.

Cytisus purpureus atropurpureus is a fine prostrate dark purple broom for covering slopes in a rock garden. It is lovely on the sloping bank by a rock garden as is also the creamy-white *C. x kewensis* which flowers in May.

The Common or Scots Broom, *C. scoparius,* which makes a golden glory of the sheltered valleys in Teesdale has given rise to many hybrids. Cornish Cream grows up to 8 ft. tall with pale yellow flowers in July and together with Darley Dale in crimson and yellow, Firefly in crimson bronze, and Red Sentinel in deep red, it is worth a place in any garden.

Cuttings of semi-ripened shoots taken in July – August, 3 to 4 in. long with a heel of old wood, root readily in sharp sand. Make certain the soft pith is not exposed or an imperfect callous forms.

Daphne

Daphnes are invaluable shrubs for both border and rock garden. A loam soil, enriched with humus yet well drained is all my plants ask for and this I give freely for the privilege of enjoying their delicately perfumed flowers.

Daphne blagayana is a prostrate shrub which grows well with dwarf rhododendrons. The creamy-white flowers open in March and distil their fragrance whenever the sun coaxes them with its benevolence. Stones dropped on the stems encourage rooting and a vigorous spread.

The Garland Flower, *D. cneorum,* I first saw growing on the short-cropped turf of an alpine pasture. On my return home I immediately bought a specimen from the first nursery which had a pot-grown plant in stock, and this now flowers profusely every April on a sunny ledge in the rock garden. I suggest pot-grown plants for this is a shrub which resents root disturbance. The habit is prostrate so the branches should be given a stone to grow over, then the rose-pink flowers are not soiled with mud splashes. A raised position is ideal so that the fragrance so characteristic of this family can be properly appreciated. Propagation is by layering or cuttings taken during July – August into a frame.

Daphne mezereum was first recorded wild in Britain sometime during the mid-18th century. I grow the pink, white, and deep red forms, but prefer the red because it flowers before all the rest and is such a richly satisfying colour.

Outside the window, as I write, there is a *D. mezereum* in full perfect flower. Each branch is completely hidden by the deep pink, tightly packed blossom. I always plant this daphne near a much used path so that everyone who passes can enjoy the sweet scent of the flowers. A warm day or two will see the first blossoms open in late February, and in spite of snow showers my bush is still lovely to look at on the last day of March. Ultimately a mature specimen will grow to 5 ft. in height, the bushes in my garden average a neat, well-furnished 40 in.

Propagation is best effected by means of seed which germinate with greater alacrity when they have passed through the digestive tract of a bird. Otherwise they need to stratify for 12 months. The seedlings should be moved when young for

Daphne mezereum

they resent root disturbance. They can also be propagated by means of rooting cuttings taken in December, but seed is certainly the most reliable.

Desfontainea

Desfontainea spinosa is a splendid holly-like evergreen with tubular scarlet and yellow

Desfontainea spinosa

The lacecap hydrangeas with flat corymbs of flowers have a distinction not shared by the more commonly grown mop-headed varieties. *Hydrangea macrophylla mariesii* has pink or blue flowers, depending on the soil.

The flowers of *Magnolia stellata* distil an unsuspected fragrance when warmed by the April sun. Lovelier still when underplanted with *Scilla* Spring Beauty.

OPPOSITE
Given a lime-free soil, with its head in the sun and roots in cool, moist shade, *Kalmia latifolia* with its unusual saucer-shaped flowers is a most beautiful flowering evergreen for early summer.

flowers. A sheltered location, and moist yet free-draining soil is essential in my experience, but this is a shrub which will grace the best site the garden can offer. It can be propagated by seed sown in a warm greenhouse in spring.

Deutzia

Deutzias are not amongst my favourite flowering shrubs because their overall appearance is too untidy. To compensate for this habit, however, they are easily cultivated, gaily coloured when in flower and grow to 6 ft. high. The type of soil they are planted in does not seem to matter providing the drainage is free and as with most shrubs there is a wide range of varieties to choose from. Avalanche has slender branches which are hung in June with fragrant white flowers. The more exposure the shrub gets the better: a sheltered position encourages early growth which in this garden is often killed by May frost.

The deutzia known as Perle Rose has a better habit, and grows 3 to 6 ft. high depending on the richness of the soil. The pale rose flowers are brought forth with unstinted generosity. *D.* x

Deutzia scabra plena

rosea includes good forms with pink or white flowers; *carminea,* pink flushed carmine, and *grandiflora,* white and pink. *D. scabra plena* gives the gardener Pride of Rochester, a variety with double white flowers, rose purple outside which verge on the ugly to me, yet it enjoys almost universal acclaim.

Cuttings can be taken in July, 4 to 5 in. long and firming towards the base which should be inserted into a 3 sand, 1 peat compost, or 4 to 8 in. long as hardwoods in November. Pruning consists of removing old wood in winter, leaving young growths to flower the following summer.

Dipelta

Dipelta floribunda resembles, but has more character than, *Weigela floribunda* and at 8 ft. high is a shrub which commands attention especially in May when covered with pink tubular flowers flushed orange-yellow at the throat. It enjoys a limy soil. Pruning consists of pinching back surplus shoots, and a judicious removal of old wood in December. Cuttings of semi-ripened wood put into a sun frame will root by the following April.

Disanthus

I have a high regard for shrubs which colour well in the autumn, and for this reason include *Disanthus cercidifolius* in my select list. A shrub of medium height, it prefers rather than tolerates a position in semi-shade, and a moisture-retentive but not waterlogged soil. The leaves turn crimson early in October and look magnificent in association with blue-flowered hydrangeas. Propagation is by means of seed, which is not easy to obtain, or by layers.

Elaeagnus

Elaeagnus has, unfortunately, proved impervious to my blandishments, disdaining my best efforts to please in regard to soil and shelter. The combination of clay soil and late frosts, which habitually visit this area in May, prove intolerable. Eventually I decided on a fresh beginning by growing *Elaeagnus commutata* (*argentea*) from seed. This has proved very successful and the silvered leaves of this deciduous bush are such an asset to the garden that once again I am to embark on an even more ambitious programme. A well-drained strong soil and shelter from east winds are two essential requirements which the majority of gardens can provide.

The evergreen *E. pungens* has obligingly sported to give several forms with very attractive coloured leaves. *Dicksonii* with leaves laced a deep gold makes a spreading bush and a very good background to *Vinca minor* Bowles Variety.

The variety I grow as *aurea-variegata* has, like so many favourites, suffered a name change and must now be known as *maculata*. Fortunately, despite this, the grey-green leaves splashed with gold still add a touch of warm bright colour to the borders. The form known as *variegata* has foliage with a broad margin of yellow which gives the shrub an air of Victorian formality.

Embothrium

The Chilean Fire Bush, *Embothrium coccineum,* was a lunatic piece of extravagance which succeeded beyond my expectations. The first bush planted 17 years ago on what was then an exposed hillside is now a small tree 15 ft. high. The label reads *Embothrium coccineum* Norquinco Valley. Each year in June the profusion of scarlet flowers against the perfectly contrasting deep green of the leaves make me eternally grateful that, ignoring all the advice offered, we insisted on trying the impossible.

Both *coccineum,* which is identical in most respects, except hardiness, with its variety above, and *lanceolatum* are well worth a place even in the most select garden. The latter, unlike Norquinco Valley, does have its young growth cut by late frost but grows away strongly in spite of this. A well-drained soil amongst heathers will suit the species and varieties admirably. Propagation is by cuttings of firm young shoots from June to August.

Embothrium

Erica

Like the calluna, the species and varieties contained within this genus bid fair to exceed in numbers the wondrous hoards of the Khan. For soils which contain any hint of lime only *Erica carnea, E.* x *darleyensis, E. mediterranea,* whose varieties offer a wide choice but limited flowering season, and of course *E. terminalis,* which flowers in June, are suitable. In planning a heather garden make the lines flow in long informal curves exactly as for calluna, preparing the soil to receive them in the same way.

A short list would include the following. First comes *E. arborea alpina,* with splendid foliage and white scented flowers in April. Good varieties of *E. carnea* include Eileen Porter, superb in rich carmine-red blossom, but slow growing; King George, a regular dwarf with deep pink flowers opening in December; Ruby Glow with dark red blossom and bronze foliage radiating warmth in every gleam of February sunshine; and Springwood White, a superb white form and the best for general planting. All the *carnea* varieties flower from December to April and can be propagated by self layers.

My list continues with *E. cinerea,* the Bell Heather, which likes its feet in cool moist soil and head in full sun. Good varieties include C. D. Eason, deep pink; Darley Dale, red; and Eden Valley, soft lilac.

Erica x *darleyensis* contains two essential varieties for me – George Rendall and Arthur Johnson, both with long spikes of pink flowers.

Erica tetralix, the indigenous Cross-leaved Heath, is not everyone's plant. The foliage is pleasant and the flowers are carried in clustered heads. It enjoys a damper soil than most heathers. Among its varieties are *alba mollis,* a white form; Con Underwood, flowers deep crimson in July – October; and Pink Glow with grey foliage.

Erica vagans, the Cornish Heath, makes a dwarf shrublet which is in colour during the period July – October. Of the varieties available *kevernensis* is rose pink; Lyonesse, a splendid white flower with protruding brown anthers; and Mrs D. F. Maxwell, a favourite of mine, with deep cerise blooms.

I have purposely left *E. terminalis,* the Corsican Heath, until the end, for it is truly a gem of good nature, a lovable shrub of 3 ft. or more which grows in shade or full sun with careless vigour. The rose-coloured flowers open in August, fading over the autumn to a warm russet brown, making a fine adornment for the winter months. All ericas, with the possible exception of Eileen Porter, propagate readily from cuttings or layers in a peat mixture.

A well-grown specimen of *Mahonia lomariifolia* in full bloom with erect racemes of flowers almost 30 in long is a truly regal sight. Long leaves composed of up to 20 pairs of hard dark evergreen leaflets are in themselves a notable feature.

A garden with no tall shrubs or small trees lacks shape. Where space is limited choose a tree – *Malus lemoinei* is an example – which is a beautiful combination of leaf and flower.

The white blossom of
the crab apple John
Downie is of secondary
importance to the
ornamental fruits which
are displayed in
autumn. For those
willing to exchange
epicurean delights for
the aesthetic, the apples
make very good jelly.

Osmanthus delavayi is a
slow-growing evergreen
shrub whose fragrant
white flowers are a
compliment to the
burdgeoning beauty of
May.

Escallonia

Any shrub border would be incomplete unless it included one member of this family of evergreens. The greatest problem I have to contend with is which of the varieties to omit. Any soil with even a tentative protestation to fertility will support escallonia. On this clay, with suitable encouragement, they are a valuable addition to the shades of summer and early autumn.

In Cornwall and other coastal areas they make grand flowering hedges which are trimmed as required to keep them within bounds but with a view to gaining the maximum amount of flower. Cuttings taken in July – August root readily.

Apple Blossom is a dainty hybrid growing 6 ft. high with pink and white flowers and it is lovely when grown with pale blue Connecticut Yankees delphiniums. Donard Beauty is 4 ft. high and exceedingly free with its rose-red flowers over many weeks. *Escallonia* x *edinensis,* an old hybrid, grows 6 ft. tall in this garden and has bright pink flowers from early June until autumn. These look lovely with a planting of the grey-leaved pyrus as a background. *E.* x *langleyensis* is of more arching persuasion and grows 6 to 8 ft. in full exposure. The deep rose crimson of the petals seen against a golden conifer make a solace for the shortening days.

For the small garden the little *E. rubra pygmaea,* only 18 in. high with tubular crimson flowers, would not disgrace a select rock garden. Cuttings taken at any time during the summer will root readily in a sand frame.

Eucryphia

Eucryphias are better grown in a neutral to acid soil which is moist yet well drained. In August every shoot is burdened down with white flowers like that of the dog rose, but with the conspicuous boss of stamens. The laggard blooms of September fall as the foliage flames into autumn gold and scarlet. The species *glutinosa,* an erect rather military shrub, and the hybrid *nymansensis* would be my choice from a first rate list of varieties.

Euonymus

Euonymus is essentially a shrub of the autumn border, both in berries which are brilliantly different to those of any other shrub, and in beauty of the dying leaves. Be the soil acid or alkaline there is little fear of the spindle tree betraying any hint of sulky perversity.

Euonymus alatus, with corky wings on the young branches, is notable for autumn colour and its height is approximately 8 ft. *E. europaeus* drives flower arrangers to paeans of praise with its red capsules and orange seeds with an approximate height of 8 to 12 ft. *E. fortunei* Silver Queen grows as a climber on the wall of a house in a village near here. The broad, silver-margined leaves marry the warm brown of the sandstone in a most becoming manner. *E. japonicus* grows in a rather sunless border with pleasant effect, but for preference I would grow the variety *albo-marginatus* for the beauty of its white-margined leaves.

E. alatus is best increased by layers or cuttings taken with a heel of old wood in August; *E. europaeus* by means of stratified seed sown in drills in a sheltered border in spring. The others will layer easily and root from cuttings in late summer.

Fagus

The beech is such a familiar part of the landscape of the whole of the British Isles that it comes as something of a surprise to discover that it is really only a native of the southern counties. There are few gardens which can support even one specimen beech, but there are forms which are so slow growing that it is possible to enjoy in miniature at least part of the splendour so characteristic of the beech. *Fagus sylvatica cristata* has spent the last 14 years in one corner of my garden and it seems firmly determined to grow only a modest half inch each summer. The deeply lobed leaves bear little resemblance to those of the common beech but appear to be the result of a misalliance with a hawthorn.

Fagus sylvatica cuprea, the Copper Beech, always conjures up memories of summer, the grass warmed by the sunlight while in the background stands the enormous canopy of copper foliage which is flecked with purple then bronze as the breeze moves the leaves. A tree of such noble proportions needs at least a quarter of an acre to develop full beauty.

Fagus sylvatica fastigiata, the Dawyck Beech, is very erect in habit and occupies little space. To me, however, the branches are so ill placed as to appear haphazardly stuck on with glue. *F. s.*

laciniata, the Fern-leaved Beech, achieves a lightness all the year round, making a most picturesque and effective specimen tree. As the name implies the leaves are pale green in colour and are divided nearly to the mid-rib.

The Purple Beech, *F. s. purpurea,* and the weeping form, *purpurea pendula,* need the broad open sweep of fields beyond. In cloistered surroundings the leaves appear almost black making a depressing spectacle when compared to their beauty on a bright summer day in rural surroundings.

Though a lime soil suits all beech best, on my acid, rather ill-drained clay they still achieve noble dimensions well worth the space they occupy.

Forsythia

Common genus though this is, it holds a special place with that other flower of spring, the daffodil, in my affection. The only virtue absent is beauty of form, but the cascade of yellow blossom which brightens the early spring is sufficient recompense for lack of quality in other respects. All are obviously tolerant of a wide range of soils, or they would not be such a conspicuous part of the landscape from one end of the country to the other. Indeed, they are sufficiently adaptable to be used as a hedge.

Unfortunately, they are frequently pruned into a grotesque travesty of vegetation which reduces them to a degree of ugliness beyond belief, without materially improving flower production.

I prune every two or three years, but only to promote strong young shoots by removing the really old wood. Cuttings taken from June onwards root readily with little attention apart from watering.

Forsythia x *intermedia* contains the cream of the genus. For the rock garden there is Arnold Dwarf, a modest 2 ft. high by 4 ft. across, which means that in heavy rain the blossoms get soiled unless a mulch of gravel is provided. Lynwood has broad-petalled flowers of a good deep yellow and is a reliable variety making a shrub 6 ft. across by almost as much high. *F.* x *intermedia spectabilis* in its best forms is my choice always. A rich satisfying yellow blossom which is unstintingly exhibited on both old and young wood. *F. suspensa* really needs the support of a building or fence, especially in the form of *sieboldii.* It is a loose-limbed plant which is splendid on a north wall where the pale yellow petals shine to a good advantage.

Fothergilla

Fothergilla major and *F. monticola* are North American shrubs which I have difficulty in

Fothergilla major

The golden flowers of this peony are displayed against the delicate beauty of the foliage. It grows most happily in association with the old-fashioned roses.

The scent of the delightfully fragrant *Philadelphus* Belle Etoile will fill the garden on a warm July evening.

Pieris formosa forrestii accompanies the panicles of white flowers with young growths which are brilliant red. A choice evergreen for a sheltered corner in lime-free soil.

distinguishing from one another except in autumn when *major* turns yellow, whereas *monticola* has leaves of brilliant scarlet. None of the fothergillas succeed to any degree on a soil which contains lime. The white bottle brush flowers open in April and I persuade myself that those of *monticola* are slightly fragrant. My bushes after 14 years are still growing, *major* is now 4 ft. high and *monticola* 3 ft., so there is no fear of the other plants in the border being swamped.

Layering in August and September is the only successful method which I have found of propagating.

Fuchsia

I have considerable regard for the bushes grown here because of the long blossoming season. Few shrubs give so much for so little attention. In hard winters the top growth is cut back to soil level, but each spring I cut away the dead shoots to make way for the forest of young growth which breaks from ground level. Fuchsias are almost indifferent to soil type but they do thrive on the lighter loams. Cuttings taken as semi-hardwoods root easily, or pieces persuaded away from the parent bush with a few roots attached are better still.

Fuchsia magellanica comes from Chile, a vastly different climate to that of the British Isles. However, growth is vigorous up to 6 to 8 ft. high, and in the summer the shoots are decorated for months with the typical fuchsia flowers, a combination of purple-blue and red. The white form I would not plant unless my garden had room to spare.

The growth of *F. m. gracilis* is upright, the foliage delicate, but the flowers are just as freely produced even if they are smaller. *F. m. riccartonii* is probably the most widely grown of all the hardy fuchsias. In Cornwall there were hedges right across the garden in which I worked for a time.

The hybrid Mrs Popple is lovely when grown in association with Michaelmas daisies, the flowers rivalling the greenhouse-cosseted hybrids in size and they are the typical red and purple colour.

The quality of Tom Thumb is such that it has actually had a place in my rock garden for 16 years, and flowers all mixed up with the paler blooms of satureia. It reaches about 10 in. high–

a modest little bush which can be propagated by division or cuttings.

Garrya

How an evergreen shrub which displays 5-in. long grey catkins in February could be regarded as attractive puzzled me for a long time. Perseverance has its own reward, and two years ago I made a large *Garrya elliptica* the central feature of a winter corner. Now flanked on one side by *Viburnum bodnantense* which has deep pink trusses and the other by *Cornus mas,* the whole aspect is transformed. Where space permits grow the male for the long catkins, and the female for the berries. If restricted to one make it the male as these bushes present a pleasanter aspect at all times.

Garrya elliptica

Some shelter on an exposed site is essential or the leathery leaves become discoloured to a hideous brown. Cuttings taken in July – August can be rooted without undue difficulty.

Gaultheria shallon

Gaultheria

These shrubs share with heathers their antipathy to an alkaline soil. They do, however, make splendid ground cover in shade for given a cool peaty soil they quickly colonise the available space with spreading underground stems.

Gaultheria miqueliana from North America runs up the peat walls, hugging the ground with intimate affection. The white or pink berries are conspicuous for only a brief period, due I believe to scrumping mice.

The best known, because at one time it was widely planted to make thickets as shelter for pheasants, is *G. shallon*. The white flowers are inconspicuous, as are the black fruits, but the green undertone they can provide beneath deciduous trees is effective in winter.

Propagation is purely a matter of removing the self-layering branches as required.

Gaulnettya wisleyensis is the result of a cross between gaultheria and pernettya. Whether this is a happy accident or carefully contrived I do not know. It makes a compact bush of 12 to 30 in. covered in dark red berries. A peaty soil suits very well, too well in my case for now suckers are popping up yards from the parent plant.

Genista

Genistas thrive on a light free-draining soil, but are perfectly satisfactory on heavy clay. It is a versatile genus which offers a range of shrubs both suitable for a small rock garden or for the less cosseted rough and tumble of the shrub border.

Genista aethnensis makes a graceful 12-ft. high bush covered in yellow pea-like blossom in July – August. *G. cinerea* is a charming bush which is so full of deep yellow flowers in June that the branches are positively weighed down. For a long time propagation defeated me, then I discovered that cuttings taken with a heel of old wood in September rooted with about 60 per cent. success in a cold frame.

Genista delphinensis is a tiny plant which I grow in a trough garden. It is also useful for carpeting the bed under dwarf conifers and if a mulch of gravel is laid down the bright yellow flowers which open in July are not soiled by mud splashes.

A generous-hearted, neat little shrub, *G. hispanica* is well nigh indispensable for the small garden. The green branchlets make a tight hummock, studded in late May with yellow blossom. Seed sown in a pot in spring, or cuttings taken in September will provide extra plants.

Genista lydia demands good drainage but it will then make a neat shrub with arching branches up to 18 in. high; the golden flowers appear in June. *G. pilosa* makes a wire-netting-like framework of branches, ideal for covering a stone or dry bank. It is absolutely prostrate with golden-yellow blossoms in May.

Prunus Kanzan is almost spoiled by over-planting. Every other suburban garden sports a specimen, the petals a canopy of pink to cheer the city-bound community. Few shrubs show the good-natured tolerance and brilliance of colour expressed by this magnificent cherry.

Hardy hybrid rhododendrons are magnificent, evergreen flowering shrubs, so it is fortunate that so many of them are compact enough, even when full grown, to fit the small garden landscape.

Rhododendron Blue Diamond makes a 3-ft high hummock of foliage, with clusters of lavender-blue flowers opening in early spring. Lovely when planted with yellow primroses.

The characteristic racemes of deep rose flowers of *Robinia hispida* need a sun-baked wall to achieve their full beauty. A light dry sandy soil offers the most suitable medium and encourages the suckering habit.

Halimiocistus

Halimiocistus ingwersenii, a bi-generic hybrid discovered by an observant gardener in Portugal, is a shrub which is deserving of wider acclaim. Planted in a rather arid soil in full sun it will continue flowering for three or four months during the summer. The oldest plant in this garden has made a neat grey-foliaged mound 18 in. high by 24 in. across after 10 years. First year cuttings can be relied on to make a creditable crop of pure white flowers. Cuttings of semi-ripe shoots taken in summer root easily enough.

Halimium

Native of the sun-warmed lands of Spain and Portugal though *Halimium lasianthum* is, it will still suffer our climate with equanimity given a well-drained soil and full exposure to our rather

Halimium lasianthum

pallid sunshine. The smoke-grey leaves show the bright yellow flowers to good effect. Cuttings root easily if taken in July – August. I also find if the roots can penetrate under a stone or paving slab the shrub is longer lived.

Hamamelis

This is a shrub of immense value and beauty for in February the dark branches are festooned with the yellow spider-like flowers and in autumn the foliage colours, unless the weather is impossibly wet, to a deep red. I grow three bushes of *Hamamelis japonica arborea* beside the silver stems of a group of birch and most years they flower for weeks on end. The scent, so much a part of this bush, seems to be much stronger after dark so that in the bright moonlight of February I need no encouragement to take my evening walk making sure that it includes that part of the woodland.

Frost has little or no effect on the seemingly fragile blossoms. As with all winter-flowering plants, a sheltered position, together with a moisture-retentive yet free-draining soil, will be rewarded with a greater profusion of the strap-shaped, twisted-petalled flowers. The bark is useful for it provides a decoction for treating insect bites, though I have never availed myself of this added virtue.

Hamamelis x *intermedia* Jelena or Copper Beauty should always be planted so that it is lit from behind by the sun from 3 p.m. onwards. Then the petals glow copper orange and produce a heart-warming sight which delights me every March.

The quickest growing is *H. japonica*. My tallest bush is 8 ft. high and nearly the same distance across. The petals are golden yellow and the calyces purple, making a soft bicolour effect. In the autumn the leaves turn a rich copper colour.

The Chinese member of the Witch Hazel clan is *H. mollis* which claims quite rightly to be the most floriferous member, each branch becoming a picture in fragrant yellow, even in the dullest, wettest February and they continue in colour for many weeks. Perfect drainage is an essential requisite or growth slows almost to a halt. Layering of young shoots suitably placed to pull down to the ground is the easiest, indeed, the only way of increasing one's stock short of grafting. Make a tongue in the branches 8 in. or so from the tip, peg this 6 in. deep into a compost well laced with sharp sand, and leave for at least 12 months until well rooted.

Hebe

In moments of forgetfulness many gardeners still refer to hebe as veronica and, no matter what name we give them, most hail from New Zealand and are not entirely hardy in every

Hebe Autumn Glory

garden. The majority flower white or a milky blue. A well-drained, not too rich soil is the best, and in my garden shelter from the dehydrating east winds of early spring is necessary.

On first aquaintance *H. armstrongii* looks like a refined dwarf conifer until July when the branches are starred with white flowers. A deep shining gold foliage intensifies with the first frost to a glorious bronze. After 12 years on my rock garden it has reached a towering 12 in. and is a delightful dwarf shrublet which is full of personality.

Autumn Glory I grow tangled with the pink *Calluna* Camla (County Wicklow) which gives it the protection so essential in inland districts. The violet spikes open from July until the first frost to mingle with the pink spikes of heather.

With small glossy leaves, *H. buxifolia* is magnificent as ground cover under the rose Nevada, making a perfect foil to the white flowers. Ultimate height is about 24 in. with me.

Hebe cupressoides like *armstrongii* bears a strong resemblance to a cypress, only this time with grey foliage. This species makes a brave display of blue flowers against the grey back-ground of the leaves and is at its best in July. It grows to between 24 and 48 in. depending on soil.

Another very adaptable ground cover plant is *H. pinquifolia pagei* with glaucous grey leaves and white flowers in June. A neat 12 in. represents the full stature so it will fit into even a modest rock planting.

The list of hebes available is immense, but a selection would not be complete without a mention of the well-loved *H. salicifolia*. In really hard winters on a clay soil the bushes are damaged by frost and may even be cut down but they quickly refurnish themselves with new leaves in the spring. Flowering often depends on the severity of this vicious pruning, but it continues from July until autumn in most years.

Where space is limited there is a dwarf form which I grow as *nana*, but which is listed in some catalogues as Spender's Seedling. This gem is only 24 in. in height compared to the species which is 5 ft. Cuttings of hebe root so readily they almost become an embarrassment, but surplus stock finds a ready welcome in less-favoured gardens.

In spite of its name, *Rosa rugosa scabrosa* is a shrub to be desired by all those who love old roses. The pale magenta flowers are followed in September by the hips which hang like scarlet waxen cherries.

Rosa rugosa Frau Dagmar Hastrup is a rose for two seasons. The lovely single flowers appear first in June with a second crop of flowers, sparser than the first, opening just as the crimson hips are ripening.

Rosa xanthina Canary Bird is not, unfortunately, a shrub for all gardens. Where happily suited to soil and situation, however, the large flowers and finely toothed leaves make this one of the most brilliant flowering roses.

The sweetly scented flowers of the handsome rose Frühlingsmorgen look even more attractive viewed in the evening light. A well-grown bush in full bloom lit from behind by the westering sun is a memory to cherish.

Hibiscus

Hibiscus will only succeed in the most favoured, sheltered gardens, and then only if they are graced with a position in full sun. When grown as I have seen them in Malton, Yorkshire and Dover, Kent they must surely be one of the finest late flowering shrubs. My experience is confined to the varieties of *Hibiscus syriacus* which also make excellent tub plants for a patio or terrace. The variety *coelestis,* a favourite of mine, has flowers of pale violet tinged with red at the base. Blue Bird is said·to be an improvement with self-coloured, violet-blue single blossoms. Hamabo, pale pink with a deeper eye colour is an old hybrid, but one of the very best in my opinion. Woodbridge, a single rose-pink, and Snowdrift, white, give a further selection of colour forms.

Holodiscus

Holodiscus discolor ariaefolius would not command immediate attention, but I find the grey-green leaves and plumes of white flowers refreshing in the July border. Like all relations of the spiraea it makes no outrageous demands about soil provided it is well drained. Cuttings of half-mature side shoots taken at a node in July root in a 3 parts sand and 1 part peat compost.

Hydrangea

Hydrangeas are not remarkable as foliage plants as a rule, but so outrageously floriferous they command immediate attention the instant buds show colour. *Hydrangea arborescens grandiflora* at 5 ft. vies with *H. cinerea sterilis* in the grossness of the white balls of bloom. Both are lovely grown against a dark background of evergreens.

The blue and white flowers of *H. involucrata* on 18-in. stems provide just the right softening influence to the lustre of the orange lily Enchantment, so I mix them up like a floral salad in a bed dominated by a sombre yew.

Hydrangea macrophylla covers a large and varied group of hydrangeas, many of which are of possible hybrid origin, and may be divided into two groups, namely the hortensias and lacecaps. With all the florets sterile the hortensia group develop positive football heads of flower, the blueness of which depends on the acidity of the soil. This can be induced by applying aluminium sulphate or generous dressings of peat. Ami Pasquier, deep red; Blue Prince, blue; King George, pink; and La France, deep rose, are all quality varieties which will do well in most gardens, particularly those near the coast. All appear to grow better in the shade where the flower colours will be better preserved.

Pruning of the hortensis section should be restricted to removing the weaker branches in early spring. Dead flowers should be left on until all fear of frost has gone to protect the buds underneath. A moist soil is best, so in dry spells drop the hose pipe on the roots to give them a thorough soaking.

The lacecaps have a quality of refinement in flower that the hortensis section lack. Bluewave is my favourite. Its gay flowers against the white trunks of silver birch, dappled with the pale sunshine filtered through a canopy of leaves, are an established part of the September scene here. Bluewave is closely followed in my affections by *mariesii* which in my soil has some blue florets while the remainder stay rosy pink. I have only seen Seafoam in a sheltered garden on the Welsh coast where its blue and white flowers amongst golden conifers looked superb. An inhabitant of a corner of the woodland here for seventeen years has been *veitchii*. The dark green foliage indicates a vigour denied by the parsimonious manner with which the florets, first white then fading to pink, are produced.

The species *H. paniculata grandiflora* makes a very impressive sight in late summer, especially when the shoots are thinned to allow full development. The branches arch over with the weight of the panicles which open first to white then fade to pale pink. *H. villosa* is one of the loveliest of the late summer-flowering species with large lilac-blue inflorescences.

Internodal cuttings of side shoots will root in sandy compost with most varieties. With *paniculata,* however, layering of the previous year's growth offers the more reliable increase.

Hypericum

Some plants radiate a positive bonhomie, and in this respect St John's Wort has few equals. In the old herbals it is credited with the ability to cure melancholy, so the prudent gardener should always have a bush on hand, at least on budget days! Just as good-natured people are usually

Hypericum patulum Hidcote

called upon for all the arduous chores, so do we tend to take advantage of plants like hypericum which will grow in the least salubrious corner of the garden. The golden-yellow flowers appear during the late summer through into autumn and provide a bold splash of colour to add a change of tone to the blues and reds of Michaelmas daisies or dahlias.

Amongst the species *H. androsaemum* is quite exceptional. It will endure shade well if no other position offers and looks very good when planted in close proximity to the red-berried *Viburnum opulus compactum*. The St John's Wort grows to 2 to 3 ft. high while the viburnum is 4 ft.

The Rose of Sharon, *H. calycinum,* is useful only to hold dry banks in place providing it can be kept from taking over the whole garden. I clip bushes in my own garden hard back before the seed ripens, and it does splendid duty as ground cover in front of laurel.

With *H. calycinum* as one parent, *H.* x *moserianum* has the vigorous but not quite the colonising property of that species. Growing 18 in. in height, the habit is dwarfer but the yellow flowers are large at up to 2 in. across.

The various forms of *H. patulum* provide the gems of the genus with *henryi* the first to flower. Growth is strong, upright, up to 4 ft., with the individual golden-yellow flowers, 2 in. in diameter, opening in succession from July into late autumn when the leaves turn bronzed purple.

Hidcote would be my choice were I restricted to one representative of the genus. Though the ultimate height can reach a rather overpowering

6 ft. with moderate or severe pruning this can be adjusted to fit within a prescribed planting pattern. The golden-yellow flowers, each with a paler boss of stamens, glow as if polished even on the dullest day. Rowallane grows only in the warmest corner, a lovely plant with cupped flowers 2½ in. across, of perfect shape and texture; a tender, delicate beauty who despises the dankness of winter so much she would rather die than endure it.

The species propagate readily from seed or pieces sliced off with a sharp spade. Named varieties can be increased by division or cuttings of semi-hardwood side shoots in August. Pruning is restricted to thinning and heading back as desired.

Ilex

The quality of the species and varieties contained in this genus, especially the evergreen members, undoubtedly makes it one of the most useful available to the gardener. Few would deny the beauty of the common holly in winter garb, of glossy green leaf and scarlet berry seen against a white landscape. They will grow in most soils, except those which are badly drained, and do not mind extremely shady conditions.

One of the most erect forms I grow is *Ilex aquifolium camelliaefolia*. The smooth, dark green leaves are almost spineless, and when mature the berries are produced in abundance.

Few evergreens can compete in beauty of berry with our common holly, *I. aquifolium,* and the many varieties related to it. Golden King with large leaves margined bright yellow confounds its given name by being female and bearing berries. By the same token Golden Queen is male with the normal spring leaves much narrower than those of Golden King. Madame Briot fortunately for the sanity of the gardening public has the good sense to be strictly female, berrying majestically with leaves which are margined and blotched with gold.

Silver Queen has cream-margined leaves but stubbornly persists in being male. I would consider myself a fortunate being if my garden were graced with a well-grown bush of Perry's Weeping Holly. Not only is it graceful, but the silvered leaves are bedecked in due season with scarlet berries.

Holly is amenable to clipping and pruning which means bushes can be kept to a neatness

Senecio greyii combines the beauty of grey foliage with an abundance of yellow daisy flowers over several weeks during the summer. A well drained soil and a position in full sun brings out the best in this deservedly popular shrub.

Spiraea x *bumalda* Anthony Waterer will adapt to growing in sun or shade without showing discomfort. Patterned shade brings out otherwise hidden colour tones in the dark, crimson flowers.

OPPOSITE
The Persian Lilac, *Syringa persica*, makes up for having smaller panicles of flowers by their quantity and intensity of fragrance. A 6-ft high bush in vigorous and healthy bloom makes a considerable contribution to the garden in May.

beyond ordinary. Seed of the species sown in the open ground after stratification germinates readily. Layering is the best method of increase for named varieties, usually performed in October. Cuttings taken in July root with a worthwhile percentage provided adequate attention is given to watering in hot weather.

Jasminum nudiflorum

Jasminum

This is a magnificent family which includes the lovely winter-flowering *Jasminum nudiflorum*. I always grow this as a wall plant and the long rambling shoots are then displayed to the proper effect. A pergola, stump, even an old stone gate post are all methods I have adopted as support and pressed into service when no wall space could be provided. As a free-growing shrub the shoots should be hard pruned to encourage a proliferation of side branches but this to a certain extent spoils the character. Flowers are produced from the leaf axils in February through to April and are a deep rich yellow and delicately fragrant. Pruning is restricted to cutting back each flowering shoot in April to within two buds of the base.

Jasminum officinale, the white-flowering fragrant climber, is rather more demanding, though it becomes a strong vigorous climber capable of covering a 12-ft. high wall with ease. Propagation of both species is easily effected by means of semi-hardwood cuttings in July – August.

Kalmia

Like the rhododendron, kalmia is a shrub which resents a soil with the slightest trace of lime. Given a medium to their liking, they make shapely evergreen bushes, 4 to 6 ft. high in the case of *Kalmia latifolia*, the Calico Bush. The bright pink flowers which are exquisitely formed with deep pink stamens merit close appreciation. Pruning consists of removing the dead flower heads.

Smaller in every way *K. angustifolia*, Sheep Laurel, makes a suckering shrublet up to 30 in. in height in the form *rubra* and is worthy of inclusion in any rock garden. Deep red flowers sit neatly in the cup of dark green leaves. Propagation is by means of cuttings or in the latter instances, self-layered shoots.

Kerria

I have a warm regard for plants which grow easily, flower profusely, and yet can be kept in

Kerria japonica

bounds without resorting to extreme measures. *Kerria japonica* will send out long arching branches up to 6 ft. in height, or sometimes 8 ft. when given a sheltered place. Whether the soil is heavy acid clay, or shallow well-drained chalk they can be relied upon to spread a creditable mantle of yellow over green polished branches.

The double-flowered form is more gaunt and less elegant. The multiplied petals have a rather artificial, manufactured look unless the shrub is carefully placed. In the right setting, against a wall or on a bank with a dark background, the yellow pompon flowers make an impressive display and give it the common name of Bachelors' Buttons.

Propagation is effected by chopping away rooted pieces from the parent or if preferred by cuttings.

Kolkwitzia

Popular names can be misleading, but in the case of *Kolkwitzia amabilis* the sobriquet Beauty Bush is thoroughly merited. Introduced from Western China at the turn of the century, this very attractive shrub has not achieved the popularity its beauty of form and flower warrant. A bush twenty years old will reach 6 ft. or rather more in height, densely furnished at the base but with long arching branches festooned in June with soft pink, bell-shaped blossoms shaded yellow in the throat. Pink Cloud is, in my

Laburnum

experience, a rather sprawling bush, but the flowers compensate for this by being a lovely shade of pink. Cuttings or layers will root if taken in September.

Laburnocytisus

Laburnocytisus x *adamii* is remarkable in that it produces flowers of three different types on the same bush. This is explained to the curious by the fact that this shrub is a result of a graft hybrid between a laburnum and cytisus. Yellow, purple and curious copper-pink blooms on one bush make for an object of curiosity rather than beauty; a personal opinion not shared by the large number of people who cherish a specimen in their garden.

Propagation is effected by cuttings taken in November, or budding in July.

Laburnum

Laburnum offers little choice except one outstandingly handsome tree in *L.* x *vossii*. In late May and early June the long golden racemes of flowers on a mature tree of 30 ft. are a truly lovely sight, especially when viewed from below under spring sunshine. A free-draining soil is essential for both this and the graft hybrid, laburnocytisus, or root development is poor. Propagation is by means of budding or grafting.

Kolkwitzia amabilis

Tamarix pentandra becomes a foam of pink flowers in late summer. To keep the shrub well shaped and compact it should be pruned in February.

Viburnum opulus nanum in full autumn livery commands the eye when lit by October sunshine. A lovely shrub to be associated with the white plumes of pampas grass.

Viburnum opulus xanthocarpum is a gauntly vigorous shrub enjoying a resurgence of popularity as a flower arranger's plant. The golden-yellow fruits, which hang in glistening clusters on the bush, add interest to the autumn scene.

Weigela Abel Carriere has purple-carmine buds which open to rose red. These look especially attractive when grown in the partial shade of a grey-leaved pear or whitebeam.

Lavandula

The word lavender creates a picture in itself of a quiet garden, warm under July sunshine, with rose beds and the paths between edged with this lovely grey-leaved, blue-flowered shrub. I used to pull the flower heads from the beds at home and tuck them down my shirt when mowing the lawn. This shrub needs care when grown on badly drained soil but presents no problems on the lighter loams.

Lavandula spica (*officinalis*) is the Old English Lavender of popular legend, but the bushes must be trimmed after flowering or it presents a rather gnarled, top heavy appearance. Folgate is a dwarf form suitable as an edging to paths or borders. Grappenhall Variety, on the other hand, makes a 36-in. high bush, and looks very well in groups down a grey and white border. Probably the most widely used of all as a hedging plant is Munstead which like Folgate grows 12 to 18 in. Hidcote, which is neat and compact, is a gem at 24 in. I do not like Loddon Pink and *rosea*, colour breaks they may be, but I prefer my lavender blue.

Liquidambar

Liquidambar has been a controversial plant in my garden for many years. It is a most un-predictable tree, handsome in its pyramidical outline and a very worthy inhabitant of the garden if only it would condescend to colour every year. Mine are threatened with eviction at regular intervals, yet when the maple-like leaves do turn the rich reds and purples that the catalogues indicate they should, all past sins are forgiven.

I have only grown the form *Liquidambar formosana monticola* which was introduced by that eminent botanist E. H. Wilson. The four specimens are planted in a well-drained though heavy soil and although last year the three-lobed leaves coloured beautifully, the year before only a barely discernable blush mantled the maiden green before the leaves fell.

Liriodendron

Liriodendron tulipifera is better known as the Tulip Tree and it is readily identified by the characteristically shaped three-lobed leaves which look as if they had been clipped short with a pair of scissors. It is certainly not a tree for the small garden for it grows quite quickly to a considerable height. A sheltered corner is essential or all the beauty of leaf is lost to the tearing bruising wind. In September – October the green fades to soft yellow as the leaves fall at the onslaught of winter. I have only seen the rather peculiar green, orange-blotched flowers at rare intervals, and would rather it refrained completely.

Liriodendron tulipifera

The variety known as *fastigiatum* or *pyramidale* offers hope to the small garden for in this case all the growth is severely upright and not spreading.

Lithospermum

The lovely blue-flowered shrubby borage has established itself firmly in my affections. Indeed, one could not help but admire the grey-green mat of leaves garnished for months in summer with blue blossom. The forms of *Lithospermum diffusum* listed as Heavenly Blue and Grace Ward make excellent rock garden shrublets, the latter having the slightly larger flowers but less robust constitution. A lime-free poor stony soil has proved the most suitable root medium in my garden; given a rich soil the growth is too lush and consequently suffers severe frost damage. In any soil it is advisable to take cuttings after six years or so for lithospermums are not particularly long lived. Taken in July and August these root readily in pumice or a peat, sand mixture.

My tallest specimens are not more than 12 in. in height even though well manured with adulation and approbation.

Lonicera

The word lonicera is a mantle which covers both the hedging and climbing forms already mentioned but there is one species, *Lonicera syringantha grandiflora*, a rather spreading shrub with glaucous grey leaves and very sweetly scented, soft lilac-coloured flowers in June to July, qualified for mention here. Give this shrub plenty of room, for it can cover a vast area in relatively few years. It is a pleasant plant which will grow well in most soils and is easily propagated by layers when required. Indeed, it roots branches without any practical help at all rather like cornus.

Magnolia

Surely no more unique setting could be devised for this magnificent genus than the rolling fells and quiet waters of The Lake District. As if aware of this magnolias seem to flourish in the warm moist climate found there as I have never seen them do elsewhere. A deep, humus-rich yet free-draining soil with adequate moisture suits nearly all the species, but they do make an effort to grow on most soils.

Magnolia denudata, the Yulan or Lily Tree, does not take long to settle in and present the gardener with a few of the pure white, cup-shaped flowers which are so elusively fragrant that it would be almost better if they had no scent at all. Magnolias should never suffer root damage, so though pot-grown specimens may cost a little more they are worth it for the assurance of success they bring.

For general planting I would recommend *M. x soulangiana*. It is a most versatile species, the rather angular branching is strangely attractive and it achieves a unique beauty when adorned with the large white flowers, stained purple at the base. The season varies between April and May, so combine the beauty with that of a pink-flowered azalea. A mulch with leafmould or well-rotted compost is a much appreciated tonic.

The cross between *M. denudata* and *liliiflora* which produced *soulangiana* has also resulted in the introduction of the white-flowered, sweetly scented *alba,* and the supremely handsome *lennei.* The last named has enormous flowers, rose purple on the outside, white on the inner surface. Shelter is essential or both leaves and flowers are ruined by the wind.

Magnolia stellata will be found to fit more readily into the small garden landscape. It flowers at an early age but so early in the year that the youthful promise can be destroyed by the black-fingered frost. A little shelter for this precocious shrub, a planting of spring bulbs and hellebore for company and spring will be ushered in with a suitable entourage.

In most cases spring layering is the best method of propagation. The soil should be well prepared with leafmould and sharp sand. I have never dared to prune my plants, resenting as they do the inference that they are not perfect it would be treated as an imposition.

Mahonia

These are delightful evergreen shrubs with handsome leaves, and in the species I shall mention, yellow flowers. They present an air of stern uncompromising endurance which I find strangely attractive. The species *Mahonia aquifolium* makes a useful low-growing ground cover under taller trees, especially cherries or acers. This does not inhibit the flowering in April which later in the year results in grape-like clusters of blue-black berries. Self-layered branches will always be found ready for lifting in autumn. *M. a. undulata* is perhaps lovelier, but at 6 ft. high too tall for ground cover. *M. japonica* is so much better than *bealei* and *undulata* that for the small garden it must be the first choice. The large clusters of pinnate leaves form a nest from which emerge racemes of pale yellow fragrant flowers, in some years during February, in others March. Colour and scent in February lift the gardener in one moment from black winter to sunlit spring. This shrub will fit into almost any part of the garden with small shrubs and heathers, and can also be used as an impact point in the herbaceous border. The black berries which appear in autumn can be persuaded to grow.

Mahonia lomariifolia is a very imposing species but it is only sufficiently hardy in milder districts. The deep yellow flowers are borne during winter on long racemes.

Malus

The flowering crabs may not make the immediate appeal of the flowering cherry, but their acceptance of a wider range of soils maintains the balance between the two genera in the public opinion poll. The choice offered in the best catalogues is quite bewildering, but only those of outstanding merit should be considered for the smaller garden.

Malus floribunda has an insidious beauty which took three full seasons to impress me. Now when the umbrella-shaped tree is covered during May with fragrant shell-pink flowers, my homage is given unstintingly especially when the pink is reflected in the white of Pheasant's Eye Narcissus underneath.

I planted Katherine with misgivings, so often May pretends to be winter that I wanted nothing to do with white flowers. As the buds showed, first deep pink fading gradually to white my conversion was complete. My only criticism is that in some years they are rather sparingly displayed. Height 25 ft. with a 20 ft. spread.

Small trees with coppery-green foliage are not common but when they display dark red flowers each and every May they become nearly collectors' pieces. *M.* x *lemoinei* has copper foliage and red flowers exhibited on a rounded bush during April and early May. The hybrid Profusion, purple-green in leaf with deep red

Malus John Downie

blossoms, makes an ideal hedge and a perfect background to golden conifers. *M.* x *purpurea,* again with purplish-green leaves, is the most widely acclaimed of all the crabs and rightly so. Its deep rosy-crimson flowers are borne with a generosity that verges on profligacy, a virtue which makes this a singularly attractive tree, up to 25 ft. tall.

Of the crabs notable for fruit rather than flowers, none I have seen rival John Downie. Fruits are conical, large, yellow striped with carnival red and excellent for making the golden jelly so apt a marriage with a fresh-baked scone.

Names can make or mar a plant, so *M. tschonoskii* was off to a bad start with me, but 16 years ago a plant came as a Christmas present and now I have a neat, practically fastigiate tree 20 ft. high, which in autumn turns into a pillar of scarlet as the leaves die. Certainly I should miss this pleasant companionable tree, not only at that season but also as the leaves open silver-grey in spring later changing to a glaucous green.

Named varieties of crab are increased by budding or grafting, or the gamblers method with species, seed sown in open beds as the fruit ripens.

Myrica

I would suspect my affection for *Myrica gale* to be coloured by sentiment, were it not for the fact that so many people admire my bush and

Above: *Olearia haastii*
Below: *Osmanthus delavayi*

early iris and similar delicate treasures. White flowers cover the 4-ft. bushes in a praise-worthy manner in August. *O. haastii,* a cosmo-politan bush and possibly the hardiest of all, has white fragrant flowers in July. The tallest speci-men I measured was 7 ft. high and grew under ideal conditions in the sandy soil of Norfolk.

Olearia nummularifolia always looks more like a hebe than an olearia to me, but botanists understand these things better than I do. Its rather stiffly erect branches, with their copper-green leaves, make a pleasant contrast in the borders to thalictrum or senecio. Cuttings of firm, current season's wood taken during October and inserted in a light, open compost root easily. Alternatively, one can take semi-hardwood cuttings in July inserting them into a sun frame.

Osmanthus

As a shrub enthusiast there are certain plants I yearn to grow well, and I go to a lot of trouble to achieve these ambitions. Now after six years of endeavour, my 4-ft. high bush of *Osmanthus delavayi* has rewarded my efforts with a credit-able show of white, perfumed flowers. The dark green leaves are in themselves attractive, especially when the bush is kept well furnished by carefully pruning in May. Ultimate height depends on situation, the biggest plant I know is 8 ft. by 15 ft. Cuttings of semi-mature side shoots are a gardener's dream of easy rooting taken in July.

A holly with tiny delicately scented flowers in September baffles most visitors to this garden and yet *O. ilicifolius* is, for most of the year, a holly in all but name. The bush here is 4 ft. high after 17 years. *O. ilicifolius aureo-marginatus* is a well-formed foliage plant with deep yellow-margined leaves. Layering side branches in October is the surest method of increase with this species and its varieties.

ask for cuttings. The wood and the leaves have a pleasant aromatic fragrance, while the copper-red male catkins transform the 3-ft. bush into something quietly beautiful from March until May. I grow it with *Salix hastata wehrhahnii* whose silver catkins contrast to perfection those of the Sweet Gale.

A moist soil is essential, a rock for the roots to penetrate under is sufficient. Cuttings of self-layered branches make an easy means of spreading plants to other gardens.

Olearia

The Daisy Bush is an attractive evergreen shrub with white, or creamy-white flowers, at least in the species I shall mention. For those who garden on the coast I would consider them well nigh indispensable. A free-draining soil and a position in full exposure to all the sun available makes for a proper vegetable contentment. Near the coast *Olearia albida* makes a useful hedge to shelter

Paeonia

Tree Peonies are not usually considered easy plants, but I have nothing but the highest regard for the species. The young breaking leaves are delightfully tinted pink, yellow or bronze, while the flowers though small compared with the hybrids make up for lack of size by the quantity in which they are displayed.

Once specimens are established, self-sown seedlings abound in the borders around them. Grow them with the old-fashioned roses, and enjoy the old world atmosphere they bring together with the rather herby fragrance.

Paeonia delavayi makes a 6-ft. high bush on wet heavy clay. The deep crimson, yellow-anthered flowers, rich with the odour of cinnamon, open from June until early August, and are followed by black-seeded fruits. *P. lutea* is best represented in the form *ludlowii* which was introduced from Tibet by Kingdon Ward, and has golden saucer-shaped flowers measuring 3 in. across. A truly magnificent shrub. The Moutan Peony, correctly listed as *P. suffruticosa,* is available in a wide range of colours, but loveliest of all are the China pink forms. As with all the others shelter should be given from the east, so that the young growths, if nipped by a late frost, can thaw out before the sun reaches them. Propagation other than seed is by layering of side branches in spring.

Parrotia

Parrotia persica, so nearly related to the Witch Hazel, should always be grown free as a specimen so that all the grace of the umbrella-like branches can be developed. The squat solid strength of the plant plus the peeling bark are attractive enough, but it is the leaf colour in autumn, all crimson and gold, which makes this such a first-class shrub. On this soil colouring was not all that it should have been until in exasperation I dosed the plant, first with magnesium limestone, and then sulphate of potash. The leaf colour has improved

Parrotia persica

each autumn since then until now it is worthy of a photograph.

Penstemon

My rock garden would be considerably less colourful if all the penstemons which grow there were suddenly eliminated. Planted on well-drained mounds or rock ledges in full sun, they only suffer damage in the most severe winters, and then, if the dead wood is clipped away, new growths soon break to hide the scars. Cuttings of young wood taken in August – September are easy enough to strike.

Penstemon heterophyllus Blue Gem is more herbaceous than shrubby with me, but the erect branching system with blue tubular flowers throughout late summer is singularly attractive. *P. laetus roezlii* is more spreading in growth, up to 10 in. high with ruby-red flowers. *P. menziesii,* evergreen through all but the coldest winter, is a neat shrublet with tubular purple flowers in late May – June.

Penstemon pinifolius is a shrub only 8 in. high and as the name implies it has leaves like pine needles. The orange-scarlet flowers are carried on leafy stems in June. *P. rupicola* wanders all over a southerly slope in my rock garden, never more than 6 in. high. In June the grey-green leaves disappear under the massed ranks of deep red flowers. All the species mentioned root from cuttings of non-flowering shoots made into a sand frame during August.

Pernettya

Unfortunately, this useful low-growing race of evergreens will not accept a lime soil, but the gardener with a suitable acid medium would do well to include them in the planting, for shrubs which carry berries until flowering time comes again in the spring are not common. Most are single sexed, so a male should be planted in a group of females to ensure a healthy crop of berries. *Pernettya mucronata* will soon form a dense bush, a 5-ft. intricate tangle of suckering stems with neat evergreen leaves. White flowers in May turn to masses of berries, which depending on the variety, range in colour from dark red to purple and white. *P. mucronata alba,* in the selected forms, has splendid white fruits. Bell's Seedling, excellent in association with heathers, has extra large red berries.

Seed is one good method of increasing stocks of this plant which will grow in sun or light shade, but to obtain specimens true to type, self-layering shoots can be lifted in autumn.

Perovskia

For two years I had a plant of Motherwort, *Leonurus cardiaca,* labelled *Perovskia atriplici-folia* and my confusion on discovering the mistake will stop me committing any further careless follies of similar magnitude. The beauty of the grey foliage, near white stems, and subsequent lavender-blue flowers depends very much on the associate planting. Grown at the edge of a flagged path to intermingle with the purple-leaved *Cotinus coggygria,* the shrub achieves a certain distinction. A well-drained soil and position in full sun are two further essentials for success. Cuttings taken in June or July will root in a sun frame.

Philadelphus

The ever-popular Mock Orange will be found in the oldest, most neglected garden, still producing a crop of flowers in July when less strong-minded plants have passed on to Elysian fields, and this is sufficient evidence of the shrub's all-round adaptability. A small complaint so far as I am concerned is the lack of a really attractive

branch outline in certain instances, but a prudent removal of the old wood in February corrects this to some extent. The soil texture seems to make little difference, but they do their enchanting best on a light loam.

Belle Etoile, with chalice-like flowers blotched purple at the base upholds the family tradition for fragrance, but reaches 8 ft. high by 6 ft. across. Enchantment, with double white flowers at 7 ft. or the Manteau d' Hermine, dwarf and bushy at 4 ft. are both reliable. *P.* x *purpureo-maculatus* is a gem, the white flowers with purple centres and sweet scent open earlier than any other. Sybille has a perfume unlike the varieties mentioned, almost like that of verbena. The flowers are also stained purple. Some growers give Virginal a poor rating, but to me it is the best double-flowered variety for scent and all-round quality.

Cuttings of semi-mature side shoots in July, or hardwood cuttings in November will root with consummate ease.

Phlomis

I remember *Phlomis fruticosa* clearly from my student days growing in a sheltered corner by the main lecture hall. Unfortunately, when it had spread into a regular patriarch of a bush 4 ft. high by 12 ft. across, severe April frost killed it. This is a hazard to be taken into account when planting shrubs of tender disposition in a cold garden.

Cuttings do root relatively easily when taken in June – July into a 2 sand, 1 peat mixture, with a $\frac{1}{2}$-in. layer of coarse sand on top, so that the risk of complete loss need never arise. The rather furry grey leaves and whorls of yellow flowers which open during the summer are most

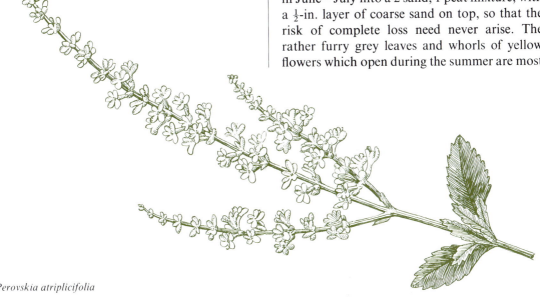

Perovskia atriplicifolia

Phlomis fruticosa

pleasant, especially in a paved corner which holds the sun's warmth.

Photinia

Photinia villosa develops an arching, umbrella habit, and makes a useful small specimen tree up to about 15 ft. high. The hawthorn-like flowers are relatively insignificant, but the autumn colour equals that of any other deciduous shrub in the garden. It shares with the quince a proneness to the disease coral spot, and needs painstaking pruning to restore it to good health.

Pieris

Pieris like rhododendrons are strongly adverse to any soil which contains even a hint of lime. Indeed, as one ericaceous enthusiast gardening on a neutral soil expressed it, even walking across his garden with a piece of chalk in his hand turned the pieris pale. Given an acid woodland type soil they make densely foliaged evergreen shrubs which deck themselves with racemes of lily-of-the-valley flowers in early spring. In some species the flowers are insignificant compared to the brilliant colouring of the young growth. The young growths open scarlet, change to pink, then pale cream before eventually acquiring the more sombre green.

The species *formosa forrestii* is very much a bird of passage in exposed gardens, but where shelter can be provided it is a magnificently furnished evergreen shrub, especially in the selected form available under the name Wakehurst. The contrast between vivid red young foliage and waxy textured white flowers is one of gardening's delightful spectacles.

Usually in my garden it is a race between *P. japonica* and *taiwanensis* as to who is into flower first. Both species reach the same height, have young growths of copper red, and are superb medium-sized shrubs. The erect panicles of flowers displayed by *taiwanensis* are more impressive than those of *japonica*. This is a race of shrubs which needs no pruning, indeed little attention, apart from a mulch of well-rotted manure or peat, and yet they will increase in beauty with each passing year.

Potentilla

Potentillas are absolutely indispensable shrubs. Amongst their virtues is the ability to grow practically anywhere in any soil except dense shade or a weeping bog. I cherish the dozen or so specimens and varieties which grow here, and enjoy the flowers which open in succession from May until September. They look a little untidy after leaf fall, but this can be forgiven in a shrub so thoroughly worthwhile. Katherine Dykes, tall at 5 ft., opens primrose-yellow flowers throughout the summer. Klondyke, a dwarf at 18 in., has sparkling golden-yellow flowers.

My own favourite, Longacre, makes a neat bush 18 in. high, and has cascades of good quality yellow blossoms. Primrose Beauty has more shape than most, with grey leaves and cream flowers. Tangerine has flowers of a delicate copper orange when grown on a lime soil in light shade and is well worth a corner.

I restrict pruning to a general thinning of overcrowded branches in March. Cuttings of

Potentilla Primrose Beauty

semi-hardwood in July are child's play to root, and I also gather up a rich harvest of self-sown seedlings.

Prunus

What can anyone who grows cherries do but wax lyrical about the mounds of blossom which erupt from every branch under the benign May sun. Brief the beauty may be, but the picture remains fresh in the mind long after the last petal falls. A deep free-draining loam is the best possible medium which can be used.

Prunus communis (*amygdalus*), the Almond, is cosmopolitan, growing as well in the town garden as it does in the cottage yard, though in the North it rarely achieves a good shape. *P. c. pollardii* has flowers of a stronger pink than the species. I grow *P.* x *hillieri* Spire in front of a 30-ft. high yew. The cherry is now 15 ft. high but still only 3 ft. across so fiercely upright are the branches but the flowers are only sparse. *P. sargentii* is beautiful in pink flower, but superb when the foliage turns scarlet in autumn. It is amongst the first to don livery in October – a tall tree at 40 ft.

Prunus tenella runs about in the rock garden attaining a modest 4 ft. in height and has bright pink flowers in May. Its variety Fire Hill has even deeper rose-pink blossom.

Of the so-called Japanese Cherries I can never have a surfeit. Amanogawa, the 'poplar' of the race, has a military erectness so useful in the smaller garden. The pink flowers which wreathe the branches are scented. Ichiyo opens shell-pink flowers later than most. Kanzan, majestic in the profusion of shell-pink full double flowers, is the most widely planted of all cherries. Cheal's Weeping is a good small specimen tree for a lawn with deep pink double blossom. Shimidsu Sakura is oriental in the superb fragile picture it makes as the pink buds open to pure white. Tai-haku, with flowers 2 in. across, is a poem of loveliness against a background of pines. Ukon, with copper-tinted leaves and cream-yellow flowers, looks magnificent with scarlet azaleas.

Prunus subhirtella has a modesty of demeanour in contradiction to the flamboyant aspect presented by the others. The best known is possibly *autumnalis,* which, whenever the temperature stays above freezing point, opens fragile white flowers. *Pendula* presents a small weeping tree with slender branches which are right in character for the smaller garden. The pale pink flowers open in early May.

*Pyracantha
coccinea lalandii*

Pyracantha

Though not in the front rank of evergreens because in an exposed garden their greenery scorches during winter to present a rather tatterdemalion-like appearance, given shelter, they are worthy of consideration. The flowers resemble those of hawthorn both in scent and shape and the bushes are not a particularly notable feature until the berries begin to ripen. Then they are a truly remarkable sight in autumn sunshine.

Of the firethorns, *Pyracantha coccinea lalandii* is deservedly the most popular. The orange-scarlet berries are large and wax like in texture and the birds devour them with avidity.

Pyracantha crenulata makes first-class greenery on a north wall, but berries rather sparsely. In full sun it ripens a good crop of fruit which is best in the form *rogersiana*. A hybrid I grow as *watereri* looks like being a notable acquisition. It is more lax in habit but well furnished in September with bright red berries.

Pruning consists of thinning the bush to shape in May, but this should be done with care or the autumn display is ruined. Cuttings taken of current season's growth in August root in a compost of 3 sand, 1 peat.

Pyrus

Pyrus salicifolia pendula makes a delightful foliage plant, for it is blessed with leaves of silver grey and is slender and elegant. With old-fashioned roses and red-leaved shrubs and a mixture of blue delphiniums, it completes one corner of my garden in a most satisfactory manner, bringing a cottage garden atmosphere of repose on a warm July day. Any soil in reasonable condition will be acceptable with no hint of condescension.

Rhododendron

A cause of infinite regret is that no member of this beautiful genus will tolerate the slightest trace of lime, no matter how disguised with peat. There are no better evergreen shrubs than the Tree Roses whose members range in height from the 30-ft. splendour of *Rhododendron sinogrande* to the prostrate posturing of *R. repens*. The evergreen species can be used as a background contrast to later flowering shrubs.

Rhododendron calostrotum is suitable for the smaller garden at 12 in. high, its grey foliage reflecting the charm of the crimson-magenta flowers. *R. ciliatum* is bud tender which means the flowers are lost occasionally. Given reasonable shelter the risk is well worth while, for the fragrant bell-shaped flowers open with those of daffodils and primroses. Ultimate height is about 4 ft.

The Alpine Rose, *R. ferrugineum,* makes a rounded bush with the young foliage copper tinted. In the best forms the flowers are a startling brick red. The grey-leaved *R. hippophaeoides* grows pleasantly out in the open in company with heathers. It grows to around 3 ft. high and its lilac flowers brighten the April days.

Rhododendron impeditum and *R. fastigiatum,* for the average gardener, can safely be classed together. Both make 18-in. high bushes with glaucous leaves surmounted by lavender blossom in April – May.

In the North *R. yedoense* is always deciduous, but otherwise commendably hardy. The habit of growth is out rather than up and it is so densely twiggy that it makes an excellent weed suppressor. The double rosy-purple flowers open in mid-May and when the shrub is deciduous a percentage of the leaves colour yellow – orange in autumn.

The list of species should include many more but the beginner would do well to plant hybrids which flower when young and accept the vagaries of our climate without discontent. Again the choice is bewildering. Both Blue Diamond and Blue Tit are dome-shaped, tightly furnished bushes with lavender-blue flowers, and are undoubtedly first class. Britannia can be positively identified by its paler leaves even without its sparkling red flowers which contrast so superbly with the Pheasant's Eye Narcissus.

Carita, cream and Carita Pink are both tall at 6 ft. Dairymaid, with compact trusses of pale yellow flowers blotched scarlet, has reached 4 ft. with me after 10 years. Elizabeth is a low-growing shrub for a peat garden and often blesses the cultivator with two crops of clear blood-red flowers, one in May and the other in August. Hawk is a neat bush flowering late in June when the season gives way to the rose. A good rich yellow-petalled blossom, it presents a strong challenge to beguile the gardener from the joys of the queen of flowers.

Lady Chamberlain, with long, narrow, bell-shaped flowers of red shading to orange, is one of my special favourites. The stiffly erect growth, sparsely leaved with glaucous green is in contrast to the more lax habits of other members of the genus.

Among the varietal forms of the hybrid *R. x loderi* are the cream of the rhododendrons, both species or hybrids. I have seen them 15 ft. high so covered in pink flowers that the colour filled the garden. My bushes after 15 years are only half that height but in flower and foliage magnificent.

Mrs G. W. Leak is so utterly reliable that no frost has yet marred the array of pink flowers, each with a purple blotch at the throat. To this must be added the ability to resist the most vicious east wind.

I use Pink Pearl with restraint. It is strong growing and with a rather loud rose-pink colour needs careful handling. A silver spruce makes a suitably subdued background. Purple Splendour flowers in June and would be worth a place for the copper colour of the young growths. The deep purple flowers are not everyone's taste and the loose and spreading habit of the branches takes up room but it looks delightful when under planted with meconopsis.

The list of evergreen azalea species, though short, has through hybridisation given rise to a positively awe-inspiring list of hybrids. Even with a garden of fifty acres it has been impossible to try them all. I list my selection under headings beginning with the best known Kurume. Addy Wery, with copper-tinted leaves and vermilion-red flowers, is a wide spreading bush which blossoms in early May. Appleblossom is altogether more relaxing with pale pink blooms flushed white. Hatsugiri is the most compact of those I grow. It has orange-purple flowers and unless it is grown amongst ferns to tone these down they are almost obscene. Hinomayo is my favourite with pale green young leaves and clear pink flowers. Snowflake, a compact shrublet with white hose-in-hose flowers colours later than the others here.

I limited the Vuyk strain from Holland to those named after musicians, growing them in groups amongst silver birch. Bach has purple flowers; Strauss, pink; Beethoven, purple with fringed petals, while Palestrina, the loveliest of all, is the exception – a delightful combination of white flushed green bought to add refinement to the rabelaisian musical hordes.

The others are a mixed bag of doubtful parentage but none the less admired. Bengal Fire I grow under a whitebeam, the fiery-orange flowers are muted by the silver above. Eddy, which is deep salmon, grows tall against the background of a steeply sloping grass bank.

All do well with a cool moist root run and shelter from late frosts and the east wind. I love to see them in open glades interspersed with the pale green and white of silver birch.

Deciduous azaleas are available by the hundred. Ignes Nova, carmine red blotched yellow, is good in autumn when the leaves turn purple. Unique is late flowering and rather tall with apricot blooms. Comte de Gomer is compact and dainty with pink blossoms. Hugo Hardyzer is 4 ft. high and a very impressive scarlet. *R. luteum* has all the qualities of a good shrub with sweetly scented yellow flowers and magnificent autumn colour. Grown amongst birch it makes a stately picture. Persil is white with a yellow blotch while Satan is blood red; Tunis is eye shattering garbed in orange-red and Whitethroat, which is dwarf in stature, has each pure white petal daintily frilled.

Named varieties are only obtained true to type from layers, and this is the most reliable method for all rhododendrons. Branches should be pulled down then tongued into the compost of peat and sand. I make certain all is secure with a heavy stone which acts as a moisture-holding mulch as well.

I do raise dozens of plants from seed, especially the azaleas, all have so far proved worth the effort. Sow in spring into a 2 peat, 1 sand compost.

Rhus

The sumachs are delightful in leaf and flower. Their cultivation presents little or no problem except in the most exposed garden with an intractable soil. The North American *Rhus copallina* has pinnate leaves which turn a rich glowing red with the first frost of autumn. Most gardeners will be well content with the Stag's Horn Sumach, *R. typhina,* which reaches 8 ft. here. The felted stems and long pinnate leaves are extremely effective. I grow it on a sloping bank surrounded by yellow-foliage plants so that the blaze of orange and purple of the dying leaves gets full appreciation. The finely divided leaves of *R. typhina laciniata* become orange and yellow in the autumn.

I usually manage to find a few suckers around the parent plant when stock for a new colony is required.

Ribes

Together with the forsythia, flowering currants are glorious plants which usher in the spring whether the days are warm with sunshine or bitter under snow. Like the forsythia I have seen ribes clipped to make a presentable hedge, but it is as a free growing shrub that most gardeners know it. Contained in the genus is one dwarf form of real merit, *Ribes alpinum aureum,* a compact bush with yellow leaves. The real gems are contained in two species, *R. sanguineum,* which has given rise to many varieties and *R. speciosum*. Of the *sanguineum* forms, *atrorubens* is notable for the

Ribes sanguineum

deep crimson flowers fully exhibited on a bush up to 8 ft. high. King Edward VII is only half that height and more relaxed in deportment with crimson flowers. Both the species and its varieties are propagated with the ease of blackcurrants by hardwood cuttings in October.

Ribes speciosum is a neat little shrub which is often mistaken for a gooseberry at first sight. Unlike the former species which will tolerate all sorts of liberties in regard to soil, *speciosum* must have a free-draining root run. In late May the pendant scarlet flowers, so similar to those of fuchsia, will hold carnival in the borders. Cuttings taken in September will root in a sheltered border or sand frame. Pruning for all species consists of thinning out the old wood every two or three years.

Robinia

In my youth I avoided planting robinias for two main reasons – the brittleness of the wood and the element of doubt about their hardiness. The robinia likes a light dry soil with a thorough baking in summer, and above all shelter from wind – three requirements no garden under my care ever possessed. Eventually, caution cast to the winds, I planted the False Acacia, *Robinia pseudoacacia,* and now my only regret six years later is that timidity deprived me of its company for so many years. The foliage has a cool elegance and the flowers in July are pale cream and faintly fragrant. In the variety *frisia* all the beauty of the species is accentuated by the rich golden yellow of the leaves throughout the summer. This is a truly lovely plant and the leaf colour intensifies at the approach of winter.

Robinia pseudoacacia tortuosa avoids the epithet curious by achieving, in spite of the distorted branches, a countenance that demands admiration. This contortion of the branches shows the underside of the leaves which is lime green to intermingle with the rich lustrous colour of the upper surface. *R. hispida* can be effectively grown against a wall.

Romneya

The somewhat exotic tree poppies can be herbaceous in severe winters, but they are so attractive when the bluish foliage is adorned with golden-stamened, white flowers that it would be a serious omission not to include them. They grow so readily from root cuttings that if one so wishes, colonies could be started in well-drained soil anywhere in the garden. *Romneya coulteri* starts to open enormous flowers 5 to 6 in. across in July, and unless maltreated continues until October. *R. trichocalyx* is lighter in foliage, more upright in habit, but otherwise for garden purposes identical.

Rosa

Many excellent books have been written on roses so that here, due to lack of space, I shall only deal with the shrub roses, without which no

Romneya coulteri

shrub border is complete. Essentially English, the rose brings the fragrance of youthful June and the grace of old world gardens and relaxes the mind as no other flower can.

Rosa alba Celestial makes a tall bush of 6 to 8 ft., grey leaved and superlatively lovely in a glory of pale pink sweetly scented flowers. *R. banksiae lutea* needs a sheltered, sun-warmed wall to show its true quality. The straw-yellow flowers are individually small yet carried in noble profusion; the soft yellow flowers are followed by dark red hips.

Frühlingsmorgen and Frühlingsgold grow to a similar height, 6 to 8 ft., and are alike in leaf and smell, but the one has cherry-red flowers centred yellow, and the other petals of palest primrose.

I grow all the forms of *R. moyesii* available and when named varieties are exhausted I experiment by growing more from seed. *R. moyesii* Geranium is more compact than most with the typical delicate leaves, orange-scarlet flowers, and flask-shaped hips, while Sealing Wax has red flowers followed by orange hips backed by the soft yellow dying leaves. Nevada with white blooms and the bud sport Marguerite Hilling with pink should also be included here for both have *R. moyesii* as parent. *R. xanthina* Canary Bird has the beauty of finely divided leaves with small canary yellow flowers in June, followed by vivid red hips.

Hybrid Musk roses form a noble clan fit company for the select border. Bonn, a gay vermilion, looks most agreeable surrounded by grey-leaved herbs. Buff Beauty is apricot yellow, but paler at the edges, a spreading bush. Cornelia is unusual in apricot, and Kassel is a suitable companion in bright red.

The hybrid Sweet Briars have scented leaves most noticable when moistened by the rain. Amy Roberts has single deep rose-pink flowers. Lady Penzance has copper flowers with yellow centres. Lord Penzance is fawn, and the semi-double Refulgence is scarlet.

The *rugosa* roses give some varieties of outstanding merit; the 8-ft. high Conrad Ferdinand Meyer with huge pink flowers, sweetly perfumed, and Sarah Van Fleet, a refined shrub of 6 ft. with pale rose-pink, camellia-like blooms redolent of a damask rose. C. F. Meyer is prone to rust fungus in some areas while there is also the lovely Frau Dagmar Hastrup.

Recent introductions which have won a firm place in my affections are Heidelberg, a strong-growing shrub which reaches around 6 ft. in height, and has double flowers of rich intense crimson, and Lady Sonia a slightly smaller delicious plant with stout branches and good deep yellow flowers.

Pruning should be done in March, removing old worn out wood and weak overcrowded shoots. Other than budding, propagation is done by means of taking cuttings of current season's growth in July and October.

Rosmarinus

Like the lavender, rosemary is loved for its old world charm, and aromatic foliage. In all but the wettest soils the height is about 5 ft. and it endures clipping sufficiently to make a hedge, as I have done utilising plants grown from cuttings of semi-ripened wood. The blue flowers open in my garden in June and the bush has been planted around with glaucous-leaved, pink-flowered dianthus so both the colour and scent can mingle.

Common Rosemary, *R. officinalis,* has given rise to several varieties, but none better than a selected form I was given from a garden in West Yorkshire called Majorca. The blossoms are lavender rather than blue, growth is upright, and if lightly trimmed after flowering it makes a dense bush which is unharmed during periods of heavy snow. A useful contrast to the species, though not quite so floriferous and slightly weaker growing is *albus.* Miss Jessop's Variety

Rosmarinus officinalis

is a good compact variety with pale blue flowers against grey-green leaves. I restrict pruning to a light trim over with the shears after flowering.

Rubus

As would be expected from a genus which contains the ubiquitous bramble, rubus will thrive in the poorest soils, even in near impossible conditions providing there is adequate raw humus, leafmould, manure, or half-rotted straw.

I grow *R. cockburnianus,* the handsome Whitewashed Bramble with silver birch and rhododendrons. The plant's suckering habit can be a problem where space is limited, as can pruning, for the same rather thorny reason. The old wood must be removed as necessary or the plant becomes a positive slum.

Rubus deliciosus is a surprise thoroughbred in the rather mustang ranks of the bramble genus. It is a thornless shrub with good foliage and large single papery-petalled white flowers produced in June.

I grow *R. odoratus* as ground cover in an open mixed wood where the large purplish, supposedly fragrant flowers are pleasant enough in June – July. I would only include it if possessed of vast acres.

Propagation of *R. deliciosus* is by cuttings in July, of the other kinds by suckers removed in spring.

Salix

The willows are usually associated with the wide sweep of water meadows and the slow restful stillness of a deep-pooled river. Few gardeners appreciate that apart from the tree forms there are low-growing varieties eminently suitable for the smaller landscape. *Salix alba tristis,* the Weeping Willow, is a familiar part of the large picture garden of poetic conception. The graceful weeping branches are lovely when sufficient space can be given for full unrestricted development. *Vitellina* is very like the above but the young shoots are yellow and the annual growth less vigorous.

The Woolly Willow, *S. lanata,* is a native plant with much to recommend it for the restricted space of the average garden. Ultimate height is about 4 ft. but though modest in stature it produces an enormous number of pale yellow catkins. The foliage provides the major interest and its common name, for it is covered in a thick mat of hairs which give a silver sheen.

Salix hastata wehrhahnii, of similar stature, makes a picture when each naked branch is studded with large pearl-coloured catkins in April. Any moist soil will support a willow even if the water content is maintained by a thick mulch of peat. Cuttings of any young shoots removed at leisure and pushed into moist earth will root with nearly one hundred per cent. success.

Senecio

Senecios are natives of New Zealand and are shrubs which I like to see in association with the stone work provided by a house wall, terrace or patio. This is possibly because the shelter and reflected warmth encourage healthier growth. *Senecio elaeagnifolius,* with thick leathery leaves felted underneath with brown indumentum, is a good shrub for the coastal garden, but needs the comfort of a wall inland. The form *buchananii* is smaller at 18 in. compared to the species 36 in., and qualifies for a place in the rock garden. The flowers are unfortunately rather nondescript. *S. greyii* makes up for its brethren's modest demeanour by making a neatly rounded bush of silver-grey leaves upon which the yellow daisy flowers sit with a modest decorum, if such a contradiction in terms is possible.

All are plants of well-drained, sun-baked regions. They root without reserve from cuttings taken at any time during the growing season, and if hard pruned break readily from ground level.

Skimmia

Skimmias resemble some rhododendrons in the neatness of evergreen growth. They will succeed in most soils as long as these are sufficiently well

Skimmia

drained to accommodate them. Until the arrival of the bisexual *Skimmia* x *foremanii* it was necessary in order to ensure a good display of berries for the gardener to sacrifice sufficient space to plant both male and female bushes. Now one bush of *S.* x *foremanii,* planted in partial shade, will supply berries in quantity on a 4-ft. bush in most seasons. I enjoy the large red berries of the species so much that it is no hardship to make room for both husband and wife. The flowers of the male are beautifully scented and carried well above the narrow green leaves. Cuttings root of current season's growth if taken with a heel of old wood in August.

Sorbus

Of this genus none can rival our native Rowan or Mountain Ash. Even when grown in some suburban gardens the deeply divided leaves and orange-scarlet berries hint of the wide reaches of moor and lonely upland loch. First, in alphabetical order must come the whitebeam, *Sorbus aria,* with leaves which are green on the upper surface and silver grey underneath. The fruits in autumn are highly coloured and irresistible so far as the birds are concerned. Two varieties are outstanding, *decaisneana* with bold leaves and enormous berries, and *lutescens* whose leaves are grey felted with hairs on the upper surface. As I have stated, though there are several dozen species of sorbus none can equal *S. aucuparia* and its varieties like *asplenifolia* which has attractive deeply divided fern-like leaves.

Sorbus aucuparia fastigiata is a form quite often seen in the wild, growing up instead of in the more normal slightly geotropic and my bushes berry enthusiastically. *Xanthocarpa* is interesting because of the orange-yellow berries. These are all forms of the well-known, scarlet-berried rowan which grows up to 35 ft. high even on a moorland hillside.

Sorbus decora nana is living proof that a name change does not mean a change in quality, for by botanist decree we must now call it *S. scopulina.* This is an excellent miniature tree up to 10ft. in height and being very fastigiate in habit it needs little room. In spring the white flowers nestle in the dark green pinnate leaves while in autumn the same foliage makes a perfect foil to the red berries.

Sorbus vilmorinii is a gem, a photographer's near-perfect subject in autumn. The growth of my plants is shrub-like up to 12 ft., and the foliage delicate and fern like, changing in autumn to deep pink. The berries also are

Spiraea x *bumalda*
Anthony Waterer

unusual in that after turning red they then change to dog rose pink.

Spiraea

Spiraeas have filled so many ugly gaps for me that it would be easy to take them for granted were they not such attractive shrubs. Most species have a graceful arching branching system, dainty foliage, and white flowers, except in the species *Spiraea* x *bumalda.* Foam of May, *S.* x *arguta,* looks like a shrubby maidenhair fern with cascades of white flowers in May on bushes 4 ft. high. *S.* x *bumalda* Anthony Waterer astonished me last year by producing cream-coloured leaves on one bush, but apparently this is not uncommon. The crimson flowers are borne on stiff upright 3-ft. high stems and are a little too prim and precise for my taste.

I like *S. japonica* best in the form *fortunei* with deeply divided leaves and bright red flowers. *S. menziesii triumphans* has grown into a formidable thicket in deep moist woodland soil here, where it continues to open panicles of deep rose flowers from July until September and to me it looks just a little self conscious in the company of the azaleas.

Propagation is by hardwood cuttings in December, or in the case of *S.* x *arguta,* half-mature side shoots 2 to 4 in. long with a slight heel, put into a compost of 2 sand, 1 peat.

Stranvaesia

For 14 years the umbrella-canopied shape of *Stranvaesia davidiana* has softened a hard line where border meets grass on the one hand, and a gravel path on the other in my garden. No doubt, with the years it will grow taller, my bushes are now some 7 ft. with narrow evergreen leaves, although a proportion do turn red in the autumn to complement the clusters of berries which are only slightly darker in colour. I have seen specimens on clay and sand, in light woodland or open border and all were charmingly attractive to the eye.

Symphoricarpos

This shrub is much loved by flower arrangers and it will grow where not even an ivy could scrape a living. In good soil it can be a nuisance. When laden with pure white large berries, *Symphoricarpos albus laevigatus* is a gift from above to the addicted flower arranger. Unless controlled, suckering will colonise the whole garden in a 6-ft. jungle. White Hedge, a more erect, less invasive form carries heavier crops of white 'moth balls'.

Symphoricarpos albus laevigatus

Stranvaesia davidiana

Syringa

Unlike the majority of gardeners I secretly prefer the species to the heavy-flowered hybrids which lack the beauty of shape or leaf to be worthy of a second look when not in flower. This may be because the species accept my acid soil with considerably better grace than the less agreeable hybrids. A neutral or alkaline soil is the ideal medium, but they do grow in well-drained acid clay. I feed each with a mixture of

3 parts bonemeal to $\frac{1}{2}$ part of sulphate of potash, at 3 oz. per sq. yd. in February.

Syringa microphylla is a narrow-leaved shrub 6 ft. high which is much lighter in the branches than most lilacs. Its pale pink scented flowers appear in May, and in most years there is a second crop in August. *S. palibiniana (velutina)* is quite distinct from the above with much rounder leaves and stiffly upright branches. The soft purple spikes are also scented. Mature specimens here are about 4 ft. high.

Syringa x *persica*, the Persian Lilac, is a charming slender-branched shrub with lilac flowers in May. Its variety, *alba*, is similar except for the white flowers.

In *S.* x *prestoniae* can be found a race of hybrids quite unlike any of the others. They are vigorous and tolerant of a vast degree of exposure and soil types. The flowers are carried in large loose panicles. Audrey, deep lilac to pale pink, has made a bush 10 ft. high in 16 years in my garden and improves each year. Royalty has violet-blue flowers and is much the same height.

I could not possibly include all the offspring of *S. vulgaris*, the Common Lilac, so will select only the best of those under my care. Among the singles there is Esther Staley, earliest to open with bright pink trusses, medium height; Etna, panicles broad and heavy, deep claret fading to washed-out pink; and Hugo Koster, purple crimson. Marechal Foch is one of the best still, with well-balanced trusses of a bright carmine rose when young. Massena is deep purple-red and one of my favourites. Souvenir de Louis Spaeth is probably the most popular of all, with dark red, well-formed spikes of flowers on long stems. These look very well against a light background provided by one of the grey-leaved sorbus.

Double lilacs are not to my taste as a rule, but Charles Joly, a dark red, is worthy of space. Edith Cavell, cream to pure white, has not the character of the other fine white, Madame Lemoine, but shows sufficient resilience to grow on very wind-swept situations. Paul Thirion, the last to flower with trusses of rose blossom fading to lilac, is like so many inhabitants of this globe, admirable when young but with a distinct tendency towards decrepitude with advancing years.

The best plants are those grown from layers in spring, but unfortunately most varieties, unless hard pruned, do not produce the right quality of wood low enough to be pegged down at soil level. Some will root from cuttings of semi-ripened shoots in July, but the task requires patience.

Tamarix

Tamarix supply a necessary contrast in vegetation down the border with their graceful slender branches, thin leaves and candyfloss inflorescences. They will not grow on badly drained soils for more than a limited period, nor will they endure a thin hot chalk, otherwise they are not hard to please.

Tamarix gallica does well on the coast, but here the shoot tips are cut back each winter by frost. Fortunately this does not stop the large panicles of pink flowers opening in June, but it does restrict the height to about 6 ft.

The tamarisks are most frequently represented in gardens by the species *T. pentandra* and *T. tetranda*. The former is late in flowering but usually mid-August sees the whole bush transformed into a foam of rosy-pink flowers – a

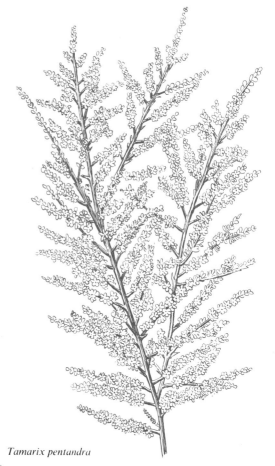

Tamarix pentandra

Ulex europaeus plenus

I first discovered the dwarf gorse *U. minor* flowering in October with calluna. Provided with a fairly arid soil, it will remain a neat compact bush with small golden-yellow flowers.

Propagation is by means of cuttings of the current season's growth, 3 to 4 in. long taken in August.

Viburnum

Viburnums must surely qualify to rank with roses, forsythia, and the other aristocrats, because they include some of the most attractive shrubs one could possibly desire for winter and spring flowering. In almost every respect the trusses are beautifully fragrant. Soil type does not seem to matter too much provided there is moderate fertility and no waterlogging.

Viburnum x *bodnantense* is a strong upright, sometimes suckering shrub which opens an unending succession of rose-coloured flowers from September until April. During periods of warm weather, the pall of winter is lifted briefly by the scent of the flowers. Dawn is one form which is consistently good with flowers a strong deep pink.

Flourishing under city smoke and the rural lane alike the cosmopolitan *V.* x *burkwoodii* has leaves which are evergreen and pink flowers which scent the air from February to April.

Viburnum x *carlcephalum* and its parent *V. carlesii* are the most widely planted of the viburnums with attractive grey-green leaves and large white globose blossoms which are richly fragrant in May.

A great favourite with me is *V. davidii* which makes a neat rounded, pleasing evergreen bush about 24 in. high. Now I have planted both male and female and instead of just getting white flowers I expect to be rewarded with a crop of turquoise berries as well. An abode in sun or full shade makes no difference to its well-being. *V. fragrans* is another which opens sweetly scented, pink-tinged flowers throughout winter. It is not quite so tall as *V.* x *bodnantense* at 5 ft. and it lacks the character necessary for a top-class shrub. There are many varieties of *V. opulus*, the Guelder Rose, with white flowers rather like those of a lacecap hydrangea and they include *xanthocarpum* which is yellow fruited.

The Japanese Snow Ball Tree, *V. tomentosum plicatum*, with double rows of flowers along horizontally arching branches in early June

truly gracious shrub. Pruned back hard in February it is more floriferous still but looses a little of its arching grace.

Native of the Caucasus, *T. tetrandra* is the species usually planted, and certainly it is very attractive when the bright pink flowers open in May. Unlike the species previously described these are carried on the previous year's growth, so pruning should be avoided so far as is compatible with the general health of the bush. Cuttings 8 to 10 in. long taken in November will root readily in light sandy soil.

Ulex

In common with many I admire the gorses which set whole valleys alight with sunshine yellow in May. Gorse is essentially informal and refuses utterly to be reduced to growing with roses and other tame plants. It should be used on hot dry banks in company with the junipers and stronger heathers. The double flowering *Ulex europaeus plenus* is the best for the close confines of the smaller garden. Never give any member of the gorse family a rich soil or it runs to flesh and fails to flower.

excites the admiration of all who see it. The dense spreading habit – a bush 10 years old will grow 4 ft. high by 6 ft. across, makes a pleasant contrast in shape even when the shrub is not in flower.

The wide-spreading horizontal branches of *V. tomentosum* look so right with grey junipers. The large flat heads of flowers are carried along the upper surface on short stalks in June. Lanarth and *mariesii* are select forms, freer flowering and in a flatter branching plane.

Self-layered branches, as I have described before, offer a bonus to the more enterprising gardener. Otherwise cuttings of semi-mature side shoots in August will be the alternative.

Vinca major

Vinca

Many years ago I discovered the good-natured appeal of the periwinkle, and have been a devoted admirer of these pleasant shrublets ever since. I did not say cultivator because once established they need little attention. *Vinca major* is the rampaging brigand, excellent on rough banks where it will open a continuous succession of blue flowers from May to September. The variegated-leaved form *variegata* should be planted as a foliage contrast. Use them under white cherry or similar spring flowering tree for all vinca are happy in shade.

Smaller in all parts except the flowers *V. minor* makes a perfect ground cover. I have seen varieties growing in the most unlikely situations and so freely do they flower with the green of the leaf so healthy that I pamper mine with good soil and only light shade. Varieties of *V. minor* with exceptional charm include *alba*, white; *atropurpurea*, deep purple; and *aureovariegata*, with leaves splashed yellow.

I would buy any plant labelled Bowles' Variety in the sure knowledge it would be worth the money. The vinca honoured with this name has a

special place in my peat garden where the large azure flowers can be seen to advantage. Close alongside is Miss Jekyll with pale yellow young shoots and cream flowers shaded pink. Rooted layers can be detached whenever anyone expresses a desire to own a plant.

Weigela

Weigelas grow best in a well-prepared soil with sufficient organic matter to provide a moist, yet well-drained root run. They are decorative when in flower, and the rather untidy character of the bush can be improved by pruning the old wood during the late winter.

The species of real quality, *Weigela florida*, like so many other worthy plants, comes from China. The flowers are rose pink outside and like pale apple blossom within and they resemble a well-proportioned digitalis. I do not approve of the variety *variegata*, as I feel it reduces the dignity of the species, but I am very much in the minority in this respect. At 4 ft. it is 18 in. shorter than the type with pale pink flowers and leaves margined cream.

The other species I treasure under the shade of a *Malus* x *purpurea* is *W. middendorffiana*. This bush at 4 ft. high is a wonderfully delicate picture when covered with pale yellow flowers, each blotched with orange in the throat.

So popular are the weigelas that quite naturally there has been a vast amount of cross breeding with a resulting plethora of hybrids. Some are recent introductions while others are already widely acclaimed. Abel Carriere is large flowered with bright rose-carmine flowers, flecked gold at the throat. Partial shade helps the colour to hold over a longer period. Bristol Ruby makes a strong growing bush 6 ft. by 6 ft. with an abundance of red flowers and it is particularly appealing when grown with a light-leaved tamarisk. Another I have grown for many years, Eva Rathke, is always worth more than a passing glance when well furnished with crimson blossom.

In the variety *lavallei* the crimson flowers are relieved by white stamens, while *styriaca* blossoms deep rose in bud opening to soft pink. Pruning on all varieties consists of cutting back each flowering shoot as the blossoms fade to within three strong buds of the base. Propagation is by semi-hardwood cuttings 4 to 5 in. long inserted in sharp sand.

Part 3

Shrubs and Trees
for various Situations

Guide to Flowering Times

WHEN MAKING a choice between the many shrubs and small trees which are easily available, the garden owner must take into consideration a variety of factors of which his soil and situation are the most important. The lists which follow are intended as a guide to the genera and species of shrubs and trees which are suitable for some of the many different soils and situations which may be encountered by the amateur gardener. All the genera and species listed have been described in the main body of the text.

Acid Soils

Though most plants will grow in a soil which is deficient in lime, there are some whose degree of specialisation restricts them to a completely acid medium. The acer is not quite so fiercely lime intolerant but all the other genera listed below sicken to a most unhealthy yellow at the first hint of alkalinity.

Acer palmatum
Calluna
Camellia
Clethra
Erica – most species and varieties
Fothergilla species
Gaultheria species
Kalmia species
Pernettya species
Rhododendron species

Lime Soils

As with acid soils, some plants are particularly suited to an alkaline-based soil. A typical example is the cytisus which on an acid clay is relatively short lived.

Buddleia species and varieties
Cytisus species and varieties
Daphne species
Dipelta floribunda
Erica carnea – lime tolerant only
E. x darleyensis – lime tolerant only
E. mediterranea – lime tolerant only
E. terminalis
Fagus sylvatica
Genista species and varieties
Hypericum species and varieties
Laburnum species

Laburnocytisus
Lavandula species and varieties
Paeonia (tree) species
Potentilla species and varieties
Prunus species and varieties
Rosmarinus species and varieties
Senecio species
Syringa species and varieties
Weigela species and varieties

Damp Soils

Amelanchier
Betula species
Carpinus betulus
Clethra

Escallonia x *langleyensis*

Cornus species
Gaultheria shallon
Myrica gale
Salix species
Spiraea species
Symphoricarpos

Dry Soils

Aesculus hippocastanum
Berberis aggregata
Cassinia fulvida
Ceratostigma willmottianum
Chimonanthus praecox
Cistus species
Cytisus species and varieties
Genista species and varieties
Hebe species
Hypericum species and varieties
Mahonia aquifolium
Phlomis fruticosa
Potentilla fruticosa and varieties
Rhus species and varieties
Robinia species and varieties
Romneya species and varieties
Symphoricarpos
Tamarix species and varieties
Ulex species

Cold Exposed Areas

Betula
Calluna
Cornus species
Cotinus coggygria
Erica
Fagus sylvatica
Gaulnettya wisleyensis
Gaultheria shallon
Kalmia
Mahonia aquifolium
Myrica gale
Philadelphus species
Salix species
Sorbus
Spiraea species
Tamarix
Ulex
Viburnum opulus and varieties

Seaside Areas

Arbutus unedo

Cassinia fulvida
Choisya ternata
Cotoneaster
Crataegus
Cytisus
Elaeagnus species
Escallonia
Euonymus
Fuchsia magellanica and varieties
Garrya elliptica
Genista
Halimium
Hebe
Hydrangea macrophylla and varieties
Ilex aquifolium and varieties
Lavandula spica and varieties
Olearia
Phlomis
Pyracantha
Rosa species and varieties
Rosmarinus officinalis and varieties
Salix
Senecio
Sorbus
Spiraea
Ulex
Viburnum

Heavy Shade

Camellia species and varieties
Elaeagnus (evergreen species)
Euonymus fortunei
Gaultheria
Hypericum species
Ilex aquifolium and varieties
Mahonia aquifolium
Rhododendron Hardy Hybrids
R. ponticum
Rubus species
Skimmia
Symphoricarpos
Vinca

The following lists giving the distinctive habits of shrubs and trees may also be helpful.

Pendulous

Betula pendula
Cotoneaster salicifolius and varieties
Malus floribunda

Prunus Cheal's Weeping
Pyrus salicifolia pendula
Salix alba tristis
S.a. vitellina

Fastigiate

Betula papyrifera
Crataegus monogyna fastigiata
Fagus sylvatica fastigiata
Liriodendron tulipifera fastigiatum
Malus tschonoskii
Prunus Amanogawa
Sorbus aucuparia fastigiata
S. decora nana (scopulina)

Specimen or Impact Plants

Aesculus hippocastanum
Betula platyphylla japonica
B.p. szechuanica
B. papyrifera
B. pendula
Carpinus species
Catalpa species
Cercis siliquastrum
Fagus species
Ilex species
Laburnum
Liriodendron tulipifera
Magnolia species
Parrotia persica
Pyrus salicifolia pendula
Sorbus aria and varieties
S. decora nana (scopulina)
Viburnum tomentosum and varieties

Variegated or Good Foliage

Acer japonicum aureum
A. negundo variegatum
A. palmatum and varieties
Berberis thunbergii varieties
Cassinia fulvida
Cornus mas elegantissima
C.m. variegata
Corylus avellana aurea
C. maxima purpurea
Cotinus coggygria foliis purpureis
Euonymus japonicus albo-marginatus
Fagus sylvatica cuprea
F.s. purpurea
Hebe armstrongii

H. cupressoides
H. pinquifolia pagei
Pyrus salicifolia pendula
Robinia pseudoacacia frisia
Salix lanata
Sorbus aria decaisneana
S.a. lutescens

Evergreen

Berberis buxifolia
B. darwinii
B. x *irwinii*
B. linearifolia
B. x *lologensis*
B. x *stenophylla*
Calluna
Camellia species
Cassinia fulvida
Ceanothus A. T. Johnson
C. Autumnal Blue
C. Delight
Choisya ternata
Cistus species
Cotoneaster franchetii sternianus
C. microphyllus thymifolius
C. salicifolius
Daphne blagayana
D. cneorum
Desfontainea spinosa
Elaeagnus pungens and varieties
Erica species and varieties
Eucryphia x *nymansensis*
Euonymus japonicus
Garrya elliptica
Gaultheria species
Hebe species
Hypericum calycinum
H. patulum
Ilex species and varieties
Kalmia species
Lithospermum species and varieties
Mahonia species
Olearia species
Osmanthus species
Pernettya species
Phlomis fruticosa
Pyracantha species
Rhododendron species
Rosemarinus
Senecio species
Skimmia species and varieties
Stranvaesia davidiana

Viburnum x *burkwoodii*
V. davidii
Vinca species

Autumn Colour – Fruit, Foliage, Stems

A great deal depends on soil type, season and exposure but the shrubs listed below are reliable and worthy of consideration.

Acer circinatum	Leaf
A. davidii	Leaf and stem
A. griseum	Leaf and stem
Amelanchier species	Leaf
Aronia arbutifolia	Leaf
Berberis aggregata	Fruit
B. dictyophylla	Leaf
B. thunbergii varieties	Leaf
B. wilsoniae	Leaf and fruit
Betula platyphylla japonica	Leaf and stem
Callicarpa giraldiana	Fruit
Ceratostigma	Leaf
Cornus species	Stem
Corylus avellana	Leaf
Cotinus coggygria	Leaf
Cotoneaster species	Fruit
Euonymus species	Fruit and leaf
Fothergilla species	Leaf
Hamamelis species	Leaf
Ilex species	Fruit
Liquidamber formosana monticola	Leaf
Malus John Downie	Fruit
M. tschonoskii	Leaf
Parrotia persica	Leaf

Euonymus europaeus

Pernettya species	Fruit
Photinia villosa	Leaf
Prunus sargentii	Leaf
Rhododendron luteum	Leaf
Rhus species	Leaf
Robinia pseudoacacia and varieties	Leaf
Rosa moyesii and varieties	Fruit
Sorbus species	Leaf and fruit
Stranvaesia species	Fruit
Symphoricarpos species	Fruit
Viburnum davidii	Fruit

Flowering Guide

The following provides a quick reference guide to the main flowering times of the genera mentioned in the A-Z Guide of Shrubs and Small Trees. Only those genera with a good

	January	February	March	April	May
Aesculus			■	■	
Amelanchier				■	
Andromeda					■
Aralia					
Arbutus					
Berberis			■	■	
Buddleia					
Calluna					
Camellia			■	■	
Caragana					■
Carpenteria					
Caryopteris					
Catalpa					
Ceanothus					■
Ceratostigma					
Cercis					
Chaenomeles				■	■
Chimonanthus		■	■		
Choisya				■	■
Cistus					
Clethra					
Corylopsis			■	■	
Corylus			■		
Crataegus					■
Cytisus				■	■
Daphne		■	■	■	
Desfontainea					
Deutzia					■
Dipelta					■
Embothrium					
Erica	■	■	■	■	■
Escallonia					
Eucryphia					
Forsythia			■	■	
Fothergilla				■	■
Fuchsia					
Garrya		■	■		
Genista					■
Halimiocistus					
Halimium					■
Hamamelis		■	■		
Hebe					
Hibiscus					
Holodiscus					
Hydrangea					
Hypericum					

flower display have been listed although some may have the added bonus of autumn berries and colour. Those shrubs and small trees whose chief display is in their berries and/or leaf colour are listed elsewhere. It must be remembered that the flowering period shown for most of the genera is covered by several species and/or many varieties.

June	July	August	September	October	November	December

	January	February	March	April	May
Jasminum		█	█	█	
Kalmia					
Kerria				█	█
Kolkwitzia					
Laburnocytisus				█	█
Laburnum					█
Lavendula					
Lithospermum					
Lonicera					
Magnolia			█	█	
Mahonia		█	█	█	
Malus				█	█
Myrica			█	█	█
Olearia					
Osmanthus				█	
Paeonia					█
Penstemon					█
Perovskia					
Philadelphus					
Phlomis					
Potentilla					█
Pieris			█	█	█
Prunus					█
Rhododendron					█
Ribes			█	█	█
Robinia					
Romneya					
Rosa					█
Rosmarinus					█
Rubus					
Salix		█	█	█	
Senecio					
Skimmia					█
Spiraea					█
Syringa					█
Tamarix					
Ulex					█
Viburnum	█	█	█	█	█
Vinca					█
Weigela					█

June	July	August	September	October	November	December

Index